CALL ME COCKROACH

LEIGH BYRNE

BASED ON A TRUE STORY

AUTHOR'S NOTE

THE FOLLOWING MEMOIR is drawn from my own personal experiences. The names, locations, exact times, and certain identifying details have been altered to preserve the privacy and dignity of the people who have passed through my life. The conversations, recalled from an imperfect memory, have been recreated in a way that best conveys the true meaning of what was said. This memoir was written to stand alone, but can also be read as the sequel to *Call Me Tuesday*, a book based on my childhood of extreme abuse. *Call Me Cockroach* covers the debilitating and often bizarre ways in which the trauma inflicted during my formative years manifested itself in my adult life. This is my truth as seen through my eyes.

*For everyone who has pushed off the bottom
and then soared to the surface
gasping for air.*

CONTENTS

ACKNOWLEDGEMENTS

SINCERE GRATITUDE GOES to my husband for sup
porting my decision to pursue writing full-time, and to
my best friend of nearly twenty-five years for helping me
to accurately recall the heartache and triumph that went
into the writing of this book. A special thanks goes out to
everyone who read *Call Me Tuesday* and encouraged me
to share the rest of my story.

THE GREAT SURVIVORS

MY DADDY ONCE called me a cockroach, because when I was a kid I dug in the trash for food scraps and drank from the dog's water to survive. He said he meant it as a compliment. Said cockroaches are the great survivors— adaptable and resilient creatures that can live without their heads for more than a month. According to him, one day we cockroaches will inherit the world.

At the time, I was only a teenager, and being compared to a filthy bug by someone I so desperately wanted to see me as beautiful was a blow to my heart and my pride. But in the years to follow, after dragging myself through more of the same toxic emotional and psychological sludge I'd been forced to crawl through as a child, I came to realize Daddy was right. If a cockroach is a symbol of a survivor, then I guess you can call me cockroach.

A NEW SHADE OF CRAZY

June, 1974

I HEARD THE CHAIN rattle as Mama slid it into its latch, and I knew that meant my bedroom door had been locked. Achy from a long day of chores, I plopped back on my bed to rest. As soon as my head landed, I noticed something was different. The plastic sheet Mama insisted I keep on my mattress—even though at twelve, my bed-wetting days had long passed—had been replaced with a crisp cotton one. This was unusual to say the least—unheard of in my world. Not once, since I was seven-years-old, had there been cloth sheets on my bed.

My knee-jerk reaction was excitement. *Mama put real sheets on my bed!* Remnants of the naïve, trusting kid I'd once been still remained, and was holding on to the hope that the hell my life had become would somehow return to something resembling normal. But the feeling was short-lived. As always, Reality, my brutal, but trusted friend, hit me smack between the eyes with a truth as painful as an arrow jutting deep into my brain. *An act of kindness from a woman who sent me to my first day of school in a paper-thin dress and no panties? A thoughtful gesture from someone who once made me wear a mask to cover my "ugly face"?* Hardly. Something was not right and I could feel whatever it was inching up my backbone.

But how can clean sheets possibly be bad? Sitting upright, I searched out the room around me for the answer. That's when I noticed a strange lump near the foot of my bed where the sheet appeared to have been plucked up to form a tiny tent. When I leaned in for a closer look, the lump moved—ever so slightly—but it was movement. I sprang to my feet. *What the heck?* For a minute, I stood there, my mind scrambling to make sense of what my eyes were seeing. "Okay Tuesday," I said. "Calm down. If you're planning on sleeping in your bed tonight you're going to have to lift the sheet and find out what's underneath." Mustering all my courage, I marched over to the bed and flung the top sheet back.

Even with all the twisted games Mama had played in the past, I was stunned by what I saw and gasped in horror. *Spiders!* —ten or more of them, some were dead, others still alive, but with broken legs, or half-mangled bodies. I jumped away from the bed and took several quick steps back, waving my hands in the air. Mama knew I was terrified of spiders. When I was about six, before she went nuts on me, one morning I was playing on our back patio and a granddaddy long-leg crawled over my bare foot. I ran into the house screaming and threw myself into the safety of her arms. I was so scared I refused to go back outside for weeks.

Paralyzed by fear, I glared at the spiders writhing around on my bed. This was a new low even for Mama—a never before seen shade of her crazy. She had to have planned her little horror show for weeks to have collected so many. I pictured her holding a jar of her captives up to a light laughing diabolically.

One of the stronger spiders began gimping toward the edge of my bed. I knew I had to do something before it got out of my sight, because I couldn't bear the thought of it creeping in unknown crevices. I searched around me for a weapon, but Mama had cleared my room of everything but my bed and a bucket for me to use as a toilet. So I did the only thing I could think of: I ripped the sheet off, trapping the spiders inside, and then dumped them onto the floor.

As soon as they tumbled out, the strong one made another valiant effort to get away, leaving me no choice but to stomp him. Some of the other spiders began fanning out in different directions, and I had to stomp them too. I continued stomping, stomping until I was satisfied all the spiders were dead. Bending to examine their squashed remains, I suddenly felt sorry for them. They were only fighting to survive like me, and I had killed them because of my fear.

I wadded the sheets into a ball and tossed them into a corner. "I don't want your stinkin' old sheets anyway!" I shouted. I could hear Mama laughing outside my bedroom door. "You're a crazy bitch!" I said. "I'll get you back for this! I won't be a kid forever! One day when I grow up I'm going to *kill* you! You wait and see!"

I collapsed on my bare mattress and cried. *What will I do when I'm finally free? Will I really kill her, or let her live and find ways to make her pay? Or will I run away as fast as I can and never look back?*

UNLOADING WORTHLESS ROCKS

Seven years later…

M AMA ARRANGED THE mimosa branches in the
vase on the headstone of Daddy's grave,, and then
took a step back to admire what she had done. "What do
you think, Ladybug?"

A sudden breeze came through the graveyard and
ruffled the fuzzy pink blooms of the mimosa, whisking
my thoughts back to an earlier, sweeter time. The flut-
tering blooms reminded me of the big mimosa tree in
the corner of the backyard of the house I grew up in on
Maplewood Drive. On my eighth birthday, Daddy built a
tree house in it for my brothers and me. I could remember
watching him as I sat nearby in the yard making a dan-
delion necklace. Once he stopped working and blew me
a kiss. Eleven years later, I could still sometimes feel his
kiss brush across my cheek.

"Well?" Mama asked.

The sound of her voice jerked me back to the grave-yard. "They're pretty, Mama."

She stepped over to Audrey's headstone and reposi-tioned a single red tulip that had fallen out of place. "My sweet baby girl," she said. "I miss her so."

As much as I had wanted Audrey to die, I missed her too. Or maybe I missed what we never had together as sis-ters. In the more than ten years since her death, I'd often wondered what things would have been like between us had she not been crippled. I pictured her standing beside me on strong, sturdy legs, holding my hand, protecting me from Mama.

Mama slapped the dirt from her hands. "I believe we're all done here," she said. "I have an idea. Why don't we go to Shoney's for a bite to eat before we head home?"

"Sure, I could go for a burger. But is Shoney's open on Memorial Day?"

"Oh, yes; seems like that place is always open these days. "See you there," she said, cheerfully, and then started for her car. We had met at the graveyard, so I knew she wanted us to drive to Shoney's separately. When we finished eating, I would head back to Nashville to Aunt Macy's, where I'd lived since I was around fourteen, and she would drive to her home in Spring Hill, a few miles away.

We were seated quickly at the restaurant. Both of us ordered ice tea to drink—Mama asked for unsweet-ened—which we sipped while we looked over the menu. I'd already made up my mind. I put in my order for a dressed burger and onion rings. The waitress stood over us impatiently tapping her pen against her order pad as Mama studied the entrees. "I'll have the country-fried steak and mashed potatoes," she finally drawled.

Ugh, mashed potatoes. I still couldn't look at them without thinking of the time Mama planted a bullet in mine just to see if I would eat it. She smeared my face in my own vomit that day and I took a hell of a beating from her too. The whole experience had been disgusting and thinking about it made me shudder.

"Tell me some more about school," Mama said, handing her menu to the waitress. "How does it feel to be a college girl?"

Already her fake kindness was grating on my nerves. "It's only a community college," I said.

"Still it's a college. At least you're going. That's more than I ever did at your age."

That was true. She had dropped out of high school at seventeen when she became pregnant with Audrey. Most girls would have toughed the year out and graduated anyway, but Mama was too proud to continue high school as a knocked-up homecoming queen.

"It's okay, I guess."

"What is it you're majoring in again?"

"Social work."

Mama emptied a second pink packet of sweetener into her tea. "What on earth made you pick that?"

Maybe it was the sugar rush from the tea. Or the saccharin she had been dishing out to me all day. Maybe I'd grown weary of her acting as if nothing bad had ever happened between us. Whatever the reason, I'd had enough. "You know why, Mama," I snapped.

"No, I *don't;* that's the reason I'm asking."

Something about the way she said the words, *No I don't,* sent me over the edge. The sarcasm in her voice, and her insistence on playing dumb insulted my intelligence. "Because of the horrible way you treated me growing up," I said, with conviction. "I want to help make sure other kids don't get treated that way."

"The way I *treated* you—*horrible?*"

Her I-don't-have-the-foggiest-idea-what-you're-talking-about tone of voice sounded authentic, but I wasn't fooled. I knew what a convincing actress she could be. Before responding, I thought about the situation. I had her pinned. Besides jumping up and darting out of the restaurant, she had no choice but to face me. No hiding behind her bedroom door this time. No hiding behind Daddy. Before me was my chance to get the answers I'd wanted for so long. To get her to admit to what she'd done to me, say it wasn't my fault, that I wasn't ugly or worthless. And most of all, I needed to know why *only me.* Why did she pick me to hate and not one of my brothers?

With newly found courage, I jumped in. "Mama, why did you treat me different than Audrey and the boys?"

"Treat you different?" She continued with the drama, with her how-could-a-sweet-little-ole-southern-girl-like-me-harm-a-fly act. "What do you mean *different?*"

"You know what I'm talking about! You remember as well as I do. There's nothing wrong with you—with your memory—only maybe it's selective.

She shifted in her seat and glanced around the restaurant. "Lower your voice, young lady; people are staring."

"Let 'em stare!" I said. "Okay, you say you don't remember? Well let me help you…"

She cut in before I could get started, "I *do* remember having some problems after my accident." With her middle finger she stroked the pink scar tissue on her cheekbone. "But I did the best I could with you kids under the circumstances."

"Yeah, maybe the fall down the stairs made you wacky for a while, but it still doesn't explain why you only turned wacky against *me*. Why *only* me?" I moved my glass of tea aside and leaned in closer to her. "You know what I think? I think the fall triggered something you already felt inside." She darted her eyes down to her tea. "Is that right Mama?"

She chased the ice in her tea with her straw. "Either way, there's no need to dredge up what's over and done with," she said.

Now I was convinced she remembered. "Over and done with? That's convenient for you, isn't it?"

She snapped her attention from her tea to me. For a second, I saw the hate resurrected in her eyes—amber, lioness eyes that had once terrified me—and for a fleeting moment, her face hovered above me, flushed and bloated with fury as she struck me over and over with the wire end of a fly swatter.

"You shouldn't talk to your mother in that tone," she said, in a controlled, authoritative voice. "What would your daddy think?"

"*Mother?* How do you have the guts to even say that? You're not my *mother!* You're the woman who gave birth to me, the woman I see once, maybe twice a year just so she can ease her guilt! You've never been a mother to me! Aunt Macy is the closest thing to a mother I've ever had!"

She nervously pushed her short hair behind her ears. "Well it's your own fault you had to leave home when you did."

"*My* fault? What was I supposed to do, hang around a place where I wasn't wanted and let you continue to beat and torture me?"

"You didn't have to attack me like... like some wild animal."

In a flash, it all came back: her skin succumbing under my fingers, the terror in her eyes, and most frightening of all—how much I enjoyed hurting her. "Maybe it's because you *treated* me like an animal!"

She shifted in her seat again. The anger lines that were etched in her face when I was a child—between her brows and around her mouth—were starting to reform. The old Mama was bleeding through the candy-coated one sitting in front of me. "I don't want to talk about this anymore. I came here to have a nice lunch with my daughter and that's what I intend to do. Now, let's change the subject."

"No, let's don't, Mama."

"Ladybug," she said, straining to soften her voice, to hold up the act. "I'm sorry you think you had a rough childhood..."

"There's another thing. Why can't you call me by my real name?"

She didn't answer; she just sat there poking at the ice in her tea. I watched her for a few minutes until what remained of my patience had vanished. I'd had my fill of the cardboard cut-out mother she had been presenting to me for the last three years, on my birthdays or whenever she felt so inclined. I grabbed my purse from the back of my chair. "Fine; if you don't want to talk about it, I'm leaving. And until you decide you're ready to face our past, I don't ever want to see you again." I half stood up from the table, then sat back down again. "Since it's obvious we won't be seeing each other anymore, I have something to tell you."

"Please, let's not talk about this anymore. Let's enjoy our lunch."

"I'm the one who killed your precious Audrey," I blurted.

For the first time, I had her attention, really *had* her attention. "What on earth are you talking about?"

"That's right; I gave her the flu that killed her. I took a piece of bubblegum right from my mouth—my filthy, germ-infested mouth—and put it in hers. The same mouth I used to eat out of the trash because you wouldn't feed me! And you know what else Mama? I'm glad I gave Audrey the flu."

"Don't say that; she was your sister!"

"She was my *half*-sister, and I loved her too, but I'm glad she's dead—she's better off dead than having to put up with your crazy ass!" I got up from the table and turned to walk away. It would have been the perfect dramatic exit—as smooth as any Mama herself could have orchestrated—had the strap of my purse not gotten hung on the back of the chair and almost pulled it over.

A few steps from the table, I ran into the waitress bringing our order. When I saw the food I almost threw up. I turned to Mama. "I don't think I could've stomached seeing you eat those mashed potatoes anyway."

"But what about your hamburger?" she said as I was leaving.

"You eat it!" I yelled back. "It won't be the first time I've missed a meal, will it Mama?"

"Ladybug, come back here!"

"I'm not your damn Ladybug!"

Walking to the car, I felt wispy, ethereal, like I'd just emptied my pockets of a bunch of worthless rocks I'd been collecting for too long. The time had come for one of us to stop the charade. I should have done it three years earlier, the first time she contacted me after I left home. But I was still full of hope then, hope that we could somehow forge a bond. I knew I could never be as close to her as most daughters are to their mothers. Too much had happened, too many grim memories, but I was willing to try for *something*. Now I realized we could never have a normal relationship—*any* relationship—because for me to be willing to try, I needed her to admit what she'd done to me and own it. I'd given her the chance and she'd refused. *It's better this way,* I thought. *Easier*

Cutting off contact with Mama meant I probably wouldn't see my brothers again. But I never saw them anyway. She'd kept us apart when we were kids and she was still keeping us apart. After daddy died, I'd heard my older brother, Nick, had gotten married, and without notice, moved to another country, estranging himself from everyone in the family, even Mama. Jimmy D. had recently graduated from high school and was considering college. Ryan was so young when I left, his face was nothing but a blurry blond-haired image in my memory. I wouldn't have known him, or any of my brothers, if I passed them on the street.

Half asleep, I could hear Aunt Macy knocking on my bedroom door and calling my name. "Tuesday… Tuesday, you'd better get up and get ready; you have to be at work at ten; don't you?"

Oh yeah, my job at McDonalds. I'd forgotten all about it. I didn't feel like going to work. I hadn't slept the night before from thinking about my argument with Mama. I lay still and pretended to be asleep, hoping Aunt Macy would go away.

Her knock became urgent. "Tuesday Leigh Storm, it's time to get up!"

She called me by my full name whenever she wanted to get my attention. She'd picked it up from Grandma Storm. Since Grandma Storm's death, Aunt Macy had taken on many of her mother's traits: whistling as she worked around the house, playing the piano regularly. She'd even started dressing like her, wearing floral patterned blouses and strings of pastel pearls.

Aunt Macy opened the door. I could hear her walking across the room toward my bed. "Get up honey," she said, rubbing my shoulder. "It's your first day on the job; you don't want to be late."

I jerked my shoulder back. "I'm coming! Give me a minute!"

"No need to get snippy with me, missy!" she said. "What's the matter? Are you sick?"

"No, Aunt Macy, I'm fine; I just don't feel like getting up right now."

"Maybe you should forget about the job and take a break this summer before going back to school in the fall."

"I don't want to quit my job, and I have plenty of time to get ready." I rolled over in bed and turned toward her. "And I'm not going back to school in the fall."

"What?"

I sat up. "I've changed my mind."

"What do you mean you've changed your mind? You were so sure social work was what you wanted to do."

"I've decided I don't want to be around abused kids. It would only remind me of what I went through. I want to forget about my past and go in a different direction."

"What brought this on?" She sat on the edge of my bed. "Did something happen yesterday between you and your mama?"

"We had it out and I told her I never wanted to see her again."

"Well that might not be such a bad idea, but don't quit school."

"I'll still go to college, Aunt Macy, I promise, but not right now, and not for social work."

"What was said yesterday? Would it help to talk about it?"

"It's not what was said, it's what *wasn't* said."

"Tuesday, you know your mama is never going to admit what she did to you. She couldn't live with herself if she did. Don't you see? It's to her advantage to forget that part of her life and she expects the rest of us to forget as well."

"All I wanted to know was why only me?"

"Have you ever thought maybe *she* doesn't know? And even if she does, is there any answer she could have given you that would've made a difference?"

What answer *did* I want to hear from Mama? Were there any acceptable reasons she could have given me for beating and torturing me, anything that would have satisfied me, put it all into perspective, made me say, Oh *that's* why you did it. Well in that case I understand.

"Why are you making excuses for her, Aunt Macy?"

"I'm not making excuses. I happen to know the injuries from her fall down the stairs were not as bad as what your daddy let on. He was hoping her concussion was an explanation for her actions. Personally I never fell for the whole amnesia thing in the first place. I think she remembers every minute of what she did. Believe me, I'm not taking up for her, I'm merely telling you what I've observed over the years about human nature. What she did to you is too awful for her to acknowledge, and the mind has its ways of protecting us from things we can't process. She's somehow managed to make it all go away, and she expects you and everyone else to go along with her, like they always have."

"Just once I wish *somebody* would admit it happened!"

"It happened, Tuesday! There!" Her eyes were watery. "And I know now from what it has done to you it must have been a thousand times worse than I could ever imagine."

"Then why didn't you do something to help me?"

"Sweetie, every day I hate myself for not doing something. There's nothing you can say that would make me feel any worse than I already do. But the truth is your grandma and I didn't know how bad your life was then. Your daddy led us to believe it wasn't a big deal. He said Rose was having some problems from her concussion and had a tendency to take her frustration about Audrey's death out on you. He told us that's why he brought you to stay with us every summer—to give her a break. Maybe we believed him because we wanted to, because we didn't want to think he'd let something bad happen to one of his children."

"But he *was* lying—to protect Mama!"

"Well then, why didn't you tell your grandma and me the truth about what was going on?"

"I'm not sure. I think I thought you already knew."

"It doesn't matter anyway because there's nothing either one of us can do about it now."

Crawling around her, I got out of bed and started digging through my drawer for some underwear. "I told Mama I gave Audrey the flu," I said.

"Not that nonsense again!"

"It's not nonsense!"

"Why'd you tell her? To hurt her?"

"No!" I slammed the drawer shut and turned around. One look at her face and I knew I was had. "Yeah, I guess you're right."

"Did it make you feel better to hurt her?"

"No; not really."

"Okay, forget about Rose for a minute. Think about you. You need to realize for yourself that you're not to blame for Audrey's death. She could have caught the flu from any one of you in the family. She probably already had it before you gave her the gum. Besides—God love her—Audrey had a bad case of polio. She had already lived longer than the doctors said she would."

Aunt Macy got up and walked to me. She took both my hands in hers. Touching was how she showed her affection, but it sometimes made me uncomfortable. "Do you want to tell me everything your mama did to you now? I may not like what I hear, but I'll listen and I promise I will believe you."

I retracted my hands. "No, Aunt Macy, I don't want to talk about it anymore. Not ever again. Silence seems to work for everybody else; maybe it will work for me too."

CHANGE ON THE HORIZON

A UNT MACY HUMMED as she prepared dinner. Even though I didn't know the name of the song, I recognized the tune because I'd heard her play it on the piano. Her skin glowed and she had a playful new spark in her eyes. She still had on the dress she'd worn to work—a simple yellow A-line she'd sewn herself. Aunt Macy had worn the same hairstyle since as far back as I could recall—chin-length wavy layers that were now gray. She was not a beautiful woman. It wasn't that she'd lost her good looks when she reached the south side of middle age, as some women do. She'd never been beautiful, even when she was younger, but like Grandma Storm, she had a chiseled, handsome face.

She was preparing what we had always called hamburger hash, a dish Grandma Storm used to make, which was a mixture of ground beef, stewed tomatoes and potatoes. Aunt Macy usually only served hamburger hash on special occasions, but it was the middle of June. Her birthday had long passed, and mine wouldn't roll around until the next month. I couldn't think of any other reason there could be to celebrate.

"Yum, hamburger hash," I said, as we sat down to the table. "Are we celebrating my birthday early?"

"No, but I do have some good news."

I became excited. "What is it?"

She picked up a butter knife and pointed across the table. "Pass me some cornbread and I'll tell you." She took a piece of cornbread from the plate, and then scooped some margarine from a tub of Blue Bonnet.

"Well, what's the good news?"

She looked over her cornbread as she buttered it and grinned like a schoolgirl. "Edwin and I are getting married!"

I swallowed hard the bite of hamburger hash I had in my mouth. Aunt Macy was in her mid-fifties, and she had been divorced for over ten years. If she was ever going to remarry, it was time. She and Edwin had been dating for more than a year now. He took her dancing, and out to eat at least twice a week. He made her happy; I could tell because she smiled a lot whenever they were together. I liked Edwin too; he'd always been nice to me. Although I was thrilled to hear of Aunt Macy's impending marriage, the thought of her having a life of her own—a life that wouldn't be centered mostly around me—made my heart drop and sent my thoughts racing. *Where will I live? Who will take care of me?*

I pushed aside my selfishness. "When?"

"We're thinking about a May wedding. Nothing fancy, just a small church service. Or, Edwin was telling me about some wedding and honeymoon package deals they have in Florida. Doesn't that sound like fun?"

"It *does* sound like fun," I said, with what felt like a sickly smile on my face.

"Aren't you happy for us?"

To keep from hurting her, I tried to feign excitement. "Yes!"

"Then come over here and give me a hug!" As we held each other, I hoped she couldn't feel my heart pounding.

"I'm happy for you, Aunt Macy, really, I am. Guess I'm shocked because I wasn't expecting the news."

"Now, of course we'll be living at Edwin's place. He has a very nice home. And you know you're welcome to live with us until you finish college and get on your feet. Edwin and I have already discussed it and he's fine with it."

Sure he is, I thought. *I'm sure he's thrilled about a soon to be twenty-year-old freeloader living in his spare bedroom.* "That's kind of him. But Aunt Macy, you forgot, I'm not going back to school this fall."

"You could change your mind... you really need to be thinking about when you're going back. Working at McDonald's won't get you very far."

"I know, I know. I promised you I'd go to college and I will, but not this fall. I need some time to decide on a new major."

That night I couldn't sleep for worrying about how I would take care of myself after Aunt Macy and Edwin were married. Even if I did move in with them, I could only stay there a short while. Aunt Macy's words rang clearly in my head: *You are welcome to live with us until you finish college and get on your feet.*

But I wasn't ready to go back to school. I wanted no part of social work, or anything else having to do with abused kids, and I couldn't think of another degree offered at the community college that interested me. Until you get on your feet doesn't mean forever. Aunt Macy had done right by me and the time had come for her to have a life of her own—a life without me in it. Before I went to sleep, I made a goal to find a way to live on my own before the wedding in May.

My job at McDonald's may not have been a viable way to support myself, but I sure did like it. The structure of working there reminded me of my childhood summers with Grandma Storm and Aunt Macy. Everything was predictable and controlled like it had been at Grandma's house. Every day I put on my uniform, stood behind a cash register and pushed buttons that read Big Mac, medium shake, and large fries. The ease of the job and the orderliness of the environment was comforting.

Sometimes I went out with my friends from work, and we did what most young people with dead end jobs and no blueprint for the future did in the 80's—we drank, cursed life, and passed around a joint while we solved the world's problems. I was particularly drawn to a girl named Sheila. She bleached her hair and went braless. She wore tight jeans and big hoop earrings that skimmed her shoulders. She drank until she was drunk and smoked pot daily. I thought she was the coolest person I'd ever met. Alcohol was the glue that bonded Sheila and me. On our days off, she would drop by with a six pack of beer. I provided the tomato juice, and we made poor man's bloody Marys, and sipped on them while we watched soap operas.

Like most young girls, Sheila thought she was invincible. She talked to strangers and took walks alone at night. She drove her car fast, while holding a beer between her thighs and putting on mascara in the rearview mirror. I, on the other hand, feared almost everything. I had no way of knowing for sure, but I believed, during my childhood, I'd bumped shoulders with Death a few times. That I'd been a breath away from drowning when Mama held my head under bathwater, or when I blacked out briefly after she'd slung me to the concrete floor of our garage. Like most people who've been brutally attacked, I'd lived the ugly truth. I knew there were sick souls with dark intentions in the world, people with flesh and bone and real hearts pounding within their chests who do the unthinkable, people who manipulate those around them and feed off control and the sense of power it brings them. And sometimes they may even be our parents. This fear had kept me safe and out of trouble while I was in high school. But now, I found myself wanting to skim my toe along the surface of danger. That's why I liked hanging out with Sheila.

On July 11, my twentieth birthday, Mama didn't call

me and ask to get together like she had on my eighteenth and nineteenth birthdays. It was a sign she had taken what I said in the restaurant seriously. *Good,* I thought.

The weekend after my birthday, Sheila, her boyfriend, Kevin, who was one of the assistant managers at McDonald's, and I went out to celebrate. To us, celebrating meant drinking, so our first stop was the liquor store.

We were sitting in Kevin's car in the liquor store parking lot waiting for him to come out with our alcohol, when a rather loud, beat up burgundy Mustang pulled up beside us. The driver, a young guy with thick, black hair that hung in ringlets around his neck, was the only one of the two people in the car I could see clearly. He seemed familiar to me, but I saw a lot of people while working at McDonald's, so I figured he was one of them.

"Either one of you old enough to buy alcohol?" he asked.

"No, but our friend, Kevin is," I said. "He's inside now getting ours."

"Think he would pick me up a six-pack? I'll give him an extra five for his trouble."

"I'm sure he won't mind," I said. "Hey, do I know you?"

"I don't know. Do you?"

"You seem really familiar to me. Do you live in Nashville?"

"No, I'm from Kentucky."

"You're kidding!" I squealed. "I used to live in Kentucky. What part?"

"Sullivan."

"Sullivan in western Kentucky?"

"Yeah, why?"

"This is weird; I lived in Uniontown for a while!"

"Did you go to Uniontown High?"

Suddenly I remembered where I'd seen him—at Uniontown Middle School. I remembered thinking he was cute, in a bad boy sort of way. "No, I moved away before high school, but I went to junior high there. That's probably where I saw you." I held my breath, praying he wasn't one of the boys who'd made fun of me because of my greasy hair, or the way I smelled, or the stupid clothes I wore.

"Sorry I don't remember you."

Thank God. "My name is Tuesday Storm. What's yours?"

"Chad Sutton." He gave me a smirky smile and narrowed his dark eyes. "Did you say your name is Tuesday Storm?"

My heart sank. *He does remember me! My greasy hair, my high-water pants. Oh my God—my smell!* I felt my face flush. "Yes," I said, sheepishly.

"That's about the coolest name I've ever heard! It's like you're a storm on Tuesday."

By this time, Kevin was coming out of the liquor store. I asked him to buy Chad some beer and he agreed to go back in for it. Chad gave Kevin some money, then leaned back in his seat and lit up a cigarette.

"So, what are you doing in Nashville?" I asked, for the sake of conversation.

"We're going to the AC/DC concert. You like AC/DC?"

"Of course," I said, trying to sound cool, even though I didn't have a clue who they were.

"What are you guys doing?" he asked.

"Just hanging out after work."

"Where do you work?"

"McDonald's across from Vanderbilt."

Kevin came out of the liquor store with a six-pack of Pabst Blue Ribbon. Chad took the beer and with a wave of his hand, drove away.

"He's cute," I said.

"I'm surprised he didn't ask you for your number," Sheila said.

"Guess he didn't like me." As I watched him drive off, something Mama had once said to me echoed in my head. *Honestly, I don't know how you're going to make it on your own. I mean I always had men standing in line to take care of me, but with your face I doubt you'll be able to find anyone.* What if she was right?

"Trust me, he likes you," Kevin chimed in. "A guy doesn't carry on a conversation with a girl past hello if he doesn't like her. He's stupid for not asking for your number. Hell, I'd ask you out myself if I didn't already have a girlfriend."

Shelia punched him in the arm. "Hey!"

"Ah, Kevin, that's sweet," I said, knowing he was only being nice.

"I mean it. You're good-looking."

Sheila punched him again.

His words made me cringe. I wasn't used to compliments and didn't know how to react to them. I couldn't wrap my head around the idea that there were people who found me attractive. Examining my reflection in the side mirror of Kevin's car, I could see why Mama had called me horse face. I had a long jaw line and cheekbones that were set high and pronounced. I'd read somewhere that bangs make your face appear shorter, so I'd recently gotten my dishwater blond hair cut in a shag. My hair had never grown to a normal thickness because Mama had pulled it out so much when I was younger. I wore my new bangs swooped to one side to cover the bald spots in front. My eyes were the only feature I liked. They were Daddy's doleful eyes, and every time I looked in the mirror I saw him. He had passed his acne on to me too, but it wasn't nearly as bad as his had been. I was okay with my body. Mama never said much about the way I was built, except that I wasn't developing like other girls my age. I still didn't have boobs, but I was tall, thin and athletic. I had a swimmers body.

No matter how others perceived me, for too many years Mama had drilled into my head that I was ugly, too many times she'd called me horse face, so regardless of the truth, ugly had become my reality. She found my face so repulsive she made me wear a mask so she wouldn't have to see it. Hundreds of men would have to tell me otherwise, hundreds of times, to even begin to silence her voice inside my head.

The following Sunday was a slow night at work. No ballgames, no buses, only the usual steady flow of customers. A regular—a sweet guy named Bart who played on the Vanderbilt football team—came in and walked up to my register. Even when there were other registers open, he always came to mine. He ordered his usual—a Big Mac, no onion, large fries and a vanilla shake. A Big Mac with no onion was a special order, so he had to wait for the crew in the back to make it. They couldn't simply take the onions off of a regular Big Mac because the manager told us some people were so allergic to certain foods that even the juices could cause them to have a reaction.

Bart was preppy cute. He had sandy blond hair, a strong jaw, the typical broad neck of a jock, and a smile that entered the room before he did. The workers in the back hated him because he messed up the flow of things in the kitchen. But I liked him because he was extra friendly to me and made a point to chit-chat while he waited for his order.

Like always, I made Bart's shake and gave it to him so he could drink it while he waited for the rest of his order. When I handed him the shake, I noticed he seemed stiff when he extended his arm. "Is everything okay, Bart?" I asked.

"Wanna go out sometime?" he blurted out of nowhere.

What? Why would he want to go out with me? He's a college guy, who attends a real college, a university, and not just any university—Vanderbilt! On top of that he's a football player! Surely I'd misunderstood what he said. While all these thoughts were racing through my mind, I stood there like an idiot and stared at Bart.

Thankfully, one of the guys in the back saved me. "Special order up," he called out. I turned away from Bart to put his food in a sack, all the while trying to figure out what I was going to say to him when I had to turn back around. One thing I knew for sure; I couldn't go out with him, and although I wouldn't allow myself to think the actual words, I knew in my heart the reason why: I wasn't good enough.

"Well do you?" he asked again.

I turned around and handed him his food. "I don't know if I can; I work almost every night," I said. "But I'll let you know." I was relieved to see there was a couple behind him getting antsy. "May I take your order, please?" I asked, using them as an excuse for looking away from Bart.

The same night, less than an hour later, another familiar face walked in the restaurant—Chad from the liquor store. With a slow, don't-mess-with-me swagger, he headed straight toward me as if he'd known ahead of time exactly where I was. "I'm picking you up after work tonight," he stated matter-of-factly. "What time do you get off?"

"Ten-thirty," I answered. It was eight o'clock then.

"I'll wait in my car."

For the rest of my shift I was a bundle of nerves to think Chad had come all the way from Kentucky to see me. At ten-thirty, I clocked out and went out to the parking lot to look for his Mustang. It was nowhere to be found. "Figures," I mumbled to myself. As I headed back inside to call Aunt Macy to come and pick me up, I heard a car horn behind me. What looked to me like a racecar—shiny blue and white, with the numbers 442 on the side—pulled up to the curb beside me. Chad was driving.

"Where's your Mustang?" I asked.

"It's at home. I brought the good car tonight." He grinned and then leaned over and opened the passenger door. "Get in."

Even though I hardly knew him, I did as he said because he didn't give me the choice to say no. He came across as being in control. I was used to control.

"Where do you live?" Chad asked, pulling out of the parking lot.

"On Westwood, not far from here."

Every so often, when the street lights whipped across Chad's face, I snuck a peek at him. He was too pretty to be a guy. Aside from the thick black hair, he had full, perfectly shaped lips, and eyelashes any girl would kill for. "Did you really come all this way to give me a ride home from work?"

"To give you a ride and get your number. I forgot to ask for it the night I saw you at the liquor store."

The first thing I noticed about Chad's personality was he didn't talk much. After about ten minutes of his monosyllable answers to my questions, and another twenty of riding around town with the stereo full blast, he said, "Better take you home now. It's a long drive back to Sullivan, and I have to work in the morning."

"Where do you work?"

"Coal mine. Where else is there to work in Sullivan?"

From my time living in western Kentucky, I knew miners made good money. That explained the nice car. "How long you been there?"

"Coming up on two years now. My dad got me on as soon as I graduated."

"Do you like it?"

"I like the money. A job's a job. Ain't too picky about what I do as long as they pay me."

"I guess you have your own place too, huh?"

"Nope, not yet. Still live with the folks, but I'm saving up so I can move out soon. For now I figure there's no sense me paying rent if I don't have to. What about you? You live by yourself?"

"Not on a McDonald's paycheck. I live with my aunt Macy."

"Where are your parents?"

"My daddy was killed in a car wreck, and my mama lives in Spring Hill, about forty-five minutes from here."

He reached over and touched my arm. I flinched as if it were the first time anyone had ever touched me. "Sorry about your dad."

"Thanks."

"Why aren't you living with your mama?"

"Long story, and there's not nearly enough time to tell it tonight. We're almost to my house."

"When did you live in Uniontown?"

"About seven years ago. I moved here in the middle of seventh grade."

"I asked around and nobody from school seems to remember you."

"I didn't get out much."

He walked me to the door and gave me a gentle kiss, like he was kissing the top of a baby's head. I dug in my purse for a pen and wrote my number on the back of his hand.

RETURN TO SURVIVAL MODE

FOR THE NEXT month and a half Chad called me every day. He drove down from Kentucky to see me on the weekends and sometimes during the week. Mostly we rode around Nashville drinking beer, and then ended the night with clumsy sex in the back seat of his car.

He didn't like me going out with my friends from work, and if I told him I had plans to, he'd say he was coming down. And he would do it too, even if he had to work the next morning, or go in on third shift at the mine, just to keep me from going anywhere without him. "I'm looking out for you," he would say. "I don't want anything to happen to you." His protectiveness made me feel cherished. Pretty soon, I got to the point where I didn't go anywhere without him because I didn't want him to worry.

One night Chad drove me to work, and as had become his habit, sat out in his car and waited for me to get off.

He parked close to the restaurant—so close I could see the fire of his cigarette get brighter every time he inhaled. Now and then he waved to let me know he was watching over me.

He'd been out there a little over three hours of my four-hour shift, when in walked Bart. He had on a yellow polo shirt with the collar turned up, and a brown bomber jacket. His jeans were the perfect tightness to show off his muscular legs without being vulgar. As he approached the counter, I hoped he'd forgotten about the whole going out thing.

"Hi, Bart!" I chirped. "Big Mac, no onion?"

"No thanks," he said. "I didn't come in to eat this time. I came in to talk to you, to ask you if you'd thought any more about going out with me."

I picked up a straw wrapper someone had left on the counter, and rolled it into a ball with my thumb and forefinger. "Well, yeah I've thought about it, but I'm kinda going out with someone now."

"No problem. You're young; you can go out with anyone you want. I only want to take you out to dinner so I can get to know you better."

He was too gorgeous to look at. His teeth were too straight, his eyes too green, and he had dimples. I loved dimples. "I probably shouldn't. The guy I've been seeing doesn't like me to go out with anyone else."

"C'mon Tuesday, it's just dinner."

Right about then the side door flew open and Chad walked up to where we were. "What the hell's going on here?"

"Just talking to a friend," I said.

"Did you tell your *friend* you were going with someone?"

"Yes! We were only talking, Chad!"

"About what?"

"I was asking her out," Bart said, defiantly. "I don't see a ring on her finger, and you don't own her."

Chad moved in close to Bart. From where I stood, their noses appeared to be touching. "Listen here, meat-head..." he said.

The night manager came out from the back. "You boys need to take this somewhere else."

Bart turned to leave and Chad followed. I knew if it came to a fist fight, Bart would kill Chad. I looked at the manager. "Can I take my break now?"

"Go ahead and clock out for the night; your shift's almost over anyway. When you get out there, get 'em away from the restaurant, or I'll have to call the cops."

Out in the parking lot, a few feet from the door they'd gone out of, Chad and Bart were squared up, face to face. Chad moved in to Bart's personal space again. "Listen here, you mother..."

"Please Chad," I pleaded. "Stop or the manager's going to call the police."

Bart turned and started walking off. "I'm outta here," he said. "I've had about enough of this redneck crap."

I was embarrassed for Chad, embarrassed for myself. Bart was a nice guy, a classy guy. As he walked across the parking lot to his car, Chad yelled out, "Don't ever mess with her again, jockstrap, or I'll kill your ass. The last guy who crossed me got a ball-peen hammer to the head."

After he'd calmed down, Chad drove us to the duck pond in Centennial Park, a place where we liked to go after I got off work. We got out and sat on the hood of his car. I was still trembling from what had happened at the restaurant. There was quiet all around us and a big gap between us.

In the limited time I'd known Chad, I'd learned if he had something to say, he said it, otherwise he didn't talk. I'd convinced myself his reticence stemmed from him being a thinker, a sensitive man who contemplated life, and his I-don't-give-a-shit exterior was a cover to protect his male ego. God only knows what Chad was thinking then, but I had one thing on my mind and one thing only—ball-peen hammers. Ever since I heard Chad tell Bart he'd hit a guy in the head with one, I couldn't shake it from my thoughts. I had to know. I took a deep breath. "What's the deal with the guy you hit with a hammer?"

"He pissed me off."

"How? What could he have done to make you so mad?"

"He was running his mouth."

I sat there a second waiting for him to elaborate, but he didn't. "Where did this happen?"

"In the parking lot behind the bowling alley in Sullivan. You know where that is?"

"Not really."

"It's about fifteen minutes from Uniontown."

"Where'd you get a hammer at a bowling alley?"

"I keep one in my car in case I need an equalizer, if you know what I mean. Here, I'll show it to you." He hopped down from the hood, opened the car door, reached in and pulled the hammer from under the back of the driver's seat. He handed it to me and the sudden weight of it caused my hand to descend.

"You hit somebody in the head with *this?*"

"Several times. The bad thing is I'm not sure if he lived through it. I got the hell out of there when I saw he was bleeding pretty bad, and haven't been back to the bowling alley since."

I stared at him in disbelief. *Who the hell are you?* "Wow! Guess I'd better not make you mad, right?"

He took the hammer back. "Baby, don't look at me like that. There ain't no reason to be scared of me. I'd never lay a finger on you. But I would defend you with my life." He put the hammer back in the car and sat beside me again, this time he moved closer.

"Want to tell me about your mom now?"

Did he just start a conversation? "It's complicated," I said. It was something I'd heard people on TV say, and I'd always wanted to say it.

"Try me; I'm pretty smart for a dumb ol' country boy," he said, chuckling at his own cleverness.

I wasn't in the mood to talk about Mama, or my abuse, but I knew I would have to sooner or later. "Basically she hated me when I was a kid. Still does, but she won't admit it."

"So ya'll don't get along."

"Well, it's more than that. She used to beat on me."

"Yeah, my old man used to knock me around sometimes when he was drinking. But not anymore; he knows I'll kick his ass now. Your mom a drinker?"

"Not really. Not in the beginning anyway."

"That leaves crazy, then."

"Yeah, that would be her."

"My old man's just a mean drunk. He's good as gold when he ain't drinking, and he hasn't been on a drunk in a long time."

"My mama did some pretty strange things to me while she was stone-cold sober."

"There ain't no reasoning with crazy."

"You got that right."

"Any brothers and sisters?"

"Brothers, but I barely know them. We weren't allowed near each other when we were kids."

"She mean to them?"

"Nope." I was beginning to understand the value of monosyllable answers.

"Hmm, strange." That was all he needed to know about my family, either because it didn't matter, or he didn't care, or in his compartmentalized world he couldn't find a way to neatly file what I'd told him away in his mind.

After a stretch of silence he asked, "Do ya love me?"

It was the last thing I expected him to say after what we'd just talked about. *Do I love you? Like I love Aunt Macy? Like I loved Daddy and Grandma Storm? Not even close.* But I loved Chad in another way, or at least I thought I did, mostly because I believed he truly loved me. And I liked the way he protected me, protected our relationship. Now we had an abuse bond.

Maybe we're kindred spirits. "I guess so," I said.

"You guess, or you know?"

"I *know*; I love you."

"I love you too then." There was a minute or so of more silence. "This driving back and forth from Sullivan to Nashville every few days is getting old," he said. "We may as well get married before I wear the tires out on my car."

He has to be joking. Why else would he ask me to marry him after having known me for only two months? Ha-ha, funny, Chad! I played along. "Sure," I said. "Why not?"

"I'm serious."

I turned to him. His eyes were black ice. I peered deep into their darkness trying to see my future.

Suddenly, I abandoned the notion of love, and my survival instincts kicked into full throttle. *Is this my answer, my way out of living with Edwin and Aunt Macy and having to go back to college?* I thought of Aunt Macy and how she deserved a life of her own with Edwin. The simple fact was I had to find a place to live and a way to take care of myself before May. *Take care of myself.* Chad wanted to take care of me, provide for me—*marry* me. Something about being around him gave me a sense of safety, yet some of his other traits frightened me. I thought of the ball-peen hammer and pictured the poor nameless man sprawled across the bowling alley parking lot, his brains spilling from his skull. *What if Chad killed that man? What if I'm sitting beside a murderer?* I thought of Bart and what it would be like to date a nice guy like him. I knew I had no business marrying Chad. Every fiber of my being told me not to. *Say no, say no, say no...*

"Sure," I said.

Chad put his arm around my shoulders and pulled me in to him. "I'll take care of you. I promise," he said, like he'd just bought himself a good hunting dog.

For someone who'd agreed to give her life away, I was unusually calm. I wasn't giddy, like a girl who was getting married should have been. The implications of what I had done had not taken hold. In my mind, I had secured my survival route.

There were no ducks visible in the pond, so I stretched out on the car hood and looked up at the starry sky. Chad joined me. Before I knew it, he'd slid a warm, calloused hand under my uniform top and the elastic of my bra, to my right breast. He gave it a squeeze. "This will soon be mine."

I tried to shove his arm back, but it lay heavy across my chest. "No, Chad, not out here!"

He laughed and retracted his hand.

A few days after Chad asked me to marry him, or rather after we agreed to get married, he called insisting I quit my job at McDonald's. He said there was no reason for me to work anymore because I'd be moving with him to Sullivan soon anyway. He had it all planned out. We would be married in Shawnee town, Illinois, where there was no blood test required, and only a twenty-four hour waiting period to be married after you get your license. After we were married we would move in with his mom and dad until he could afford to buy us a trailer.

"What's the rush?" I asked, part of me hoping for a real, white-dress wedding, instead of a quick hitch by a Justice of the Peace.

"The *rush* is I'm tired of driving back and forth… and I want us to be together all the time."

The last part was all that sunk in.

The next morning, I gave my notice to the manager at work. He glared at me dumbstruck. "You're marrying the punk ass kid that tried to start a fight here a few nights ago?"

Sheila's reaction was even worse. "You're marrying the redneck? The best-looking guy who ever walked through these doors asks you out and you turn him down to marry a hillbilly with a little man complex?"

"I thought you said Chad was cute."

"Cute, yeah, to go out with, but I didn't think you'd marry him! Nobody *marries* a guy like that."

I had hoped she would squeal and giggle with excitement for me, the way all girls do when they find out one of their friends is getting married. But her reaction didn't surprise me. I chalked it up to jealousy. Everybody knew she had been wishing for an engagement ring from Kevin for months.

That afternoon, I called Aunt Macy at work and told her I would be making dinner. "We're having hamburger hash," I said.

"Really?" She sounded intrigued. "What's the occasion? I hope it's what I think it is."

It wasn't. "It's a surprise," I said.

Over dinner, I told Aunt Macy that Chad and I were getting married. She was not at all enthused to find out. She put down her fork and pushed away her plate of hamburger hash.

"Aren't you happy for me?" I asked, feeding back to her the same words she'd fed to me when she told me she was marrying Edwin.

She furrowed her brow. She had three deep wavy lines on her forehead, like Daddy used to have when he was angry. A snapshot of his furious face the day he found out I'd told the lady from social services about the way Mama treated me appeared in my head. "No, I'm *not.*"

"I was happy for you and Edwin."

"That's an entirely different situation."

"How?"

"Because you're too young to get married. You don't even know this boy; you've barely been seeing him two months." Tears pooled in her pale eyes. "And what about college? You promised me you'd go back."

"And I will. I still have plenty of time, and I'm sure Chad won't mind."

"That boy has no understanding of the need for a college education. Does he even have a high school diploma?"

"Yes he does." I replied, defensively. "And he has a good job too, a job where he makes plenty of money to support us."

"If you go through with this, Tuesday, mark my word, you'll ruin your life."

"You don't know that! Maybe Chad loves me. Someone can love *me* you know. Maybe he'll take care of me forever."

"Maybe he will, but it's not likely. I didn't fall off the turnip truck yesterday; I know a thing or two about people."

"You can't talk me out of it by bad-mouthing Chad. I love him and we're going to be married. Besides, you deserve a life of your own with Edwin. You've taken care of me long enough."

"Is that what this is about? Taking care of you isn't a burden," she said, soothingly. "You're like my daughter."

"And you're like my mother, Aunt Macy, but I'm almost twenty. It's time I'm on my own."

"That's just it; you *won't* be on your own. Chad will be taking care of you. And if I have him pegged right, once you let him take care of you he'll think he owns you."

"You have no reason to talk about Chad that way. He's a decent, hard-working man."

She got up from the table and picked up her food, all in one motion. Then she stomped over to the sink and dropped her plate in, hamburger hash and all. She stood there for a minute, with her head bowed over the sink, as if she was afraid she'd cracked Grandma Storm's Blue

Willow china. "You're going to do what you're going to do anyway, Tuesday; I can't stop you. But I won't support you in this either- -I can't in good conscious."

MY NEW FAMILY

LESS THAN TWO weeks later, on a Sunday afternoon
in late September, I was in my room packing my
things to move back to Kentucky with Chad. I'd told him
to wait in the car because I was afraid he and Aunt Macy
would get into an argument. She stood over my shoulder,
balling. "Don't do it, Tuesday," she pleaded. "Give me the
word and I'll go out there and tell that boy to be on his
way back to Kentucky."

Seeing Aunt Macy cry broke my heart, but I had no
intention of changing my mind. I looked forward to being
a wife and living on my own like an adult, but most of all,
having no one to tell me what to do. "Aunt Macy, why are
you crying? Why can't you be happy for me? It's what I
want!"

"You don't know what you *want!* You're like a lost
puppy following anyone who shows you some attention."

"Chad's not the only one who's given me attention.
Plenty of guys have asked me out!" By plenty of guys I

meant Bart. And Kevin *said* he would've if he wasn't dating Sheila. "I chose Chad because I love him!"

She followed me to the bathroom and stood over me as I dug through the laundry hamper to see if any of my clothes were in there. "I'm going to miss you, sweetheart," she said in a fragile voice.

I turned around and looked at her standing in the doorway. Her angry tears were gone, replaced with painful ones. She had the same lost, bewildered expression on her face she had the night she walked in and caught me eating toilet paper. She'd believed in me then. Stood by me even as I turned on myself, convinced I was a hopeless freak. Nobody had understood me and loved me like Aunt Macy. Nobody. My heart lurched for her. I started crying—deep from my gut crying. *What was I doing leaving the only person I was sure loved me?* "I'll miss you too, Aunt Macy."

I was so close to backing out, so close to changing the course of my life, when Chad honked his car horn. Gathering my belongings, I ran out to him carrying an overstuffed suitcase in one hand, and dragging a plastic trash bag full of clothes behind me with the other.

"This all of it?" Chad asked, getting out of the car to help me load my things into the trunk.

"Yes, but I have to say good-bye to Aunt Macy. I'll be right back."

I went into the house, hugged Aunt Macy and told her I would call her in a few days.

"I love you, Tuesday," she said. "But if you leave here

today, you're on your own. Don't come crying back to me if it doesn't work."

The closer Chad and I got to Sullivan, the more nervous I became about meeting his family, particularly his mother. True to his nature, he hadn't told me much about any of them. All I knew was he was the only boy, and the youngest of six, and that he and one of his sisters, Trudy, still lived at home.

"Tell me about your mom," I said.

"There's nothing to tell. She's a mom."

"What's she like?" I reached over and twisted one of his black curls around my finger. "I'll bet she spoils you rotten because you're the only boy."

"Yeah, I guess she does."

"Your sisters probably do too, right?"

"I don't know about all that..."

For a minute or two, I stopped talking, hoping he would offer up something on his own without me having to ask. I thought maybe he might slip into a childhood story that would illustrate his relationship with his sisters, or relate something cute he'd told them about me, or us. No such luck. He matched my silence with his.

"So what have you told them about me?" I asked.

"I told 'em we're gettin' married; that's all they need to know." He pointed a thumb toward the back of the car. "Hand me a cold beer, would ya?"

As I fished an icy PBR from the Styrofoam cooler in the back, I saw, on the floorboard behind the driver's seat, the ball-peen hammer Chad had used to beat up the guy at the bowling alley. I reached down and shoved it from my sight. I'd learned that one from my dad; shove a problem out of sight and maybe it will go away.

After shaking the ice from the can, I offered it to Chad. "Ain't you gonna open it for me?" I pulled the tab and handed him the beer. He took a cursory check around him for cops before drinking. Then, as if the alcohol had lubricated his tongue, he said, "Mom *did* ask me why you were living with your aunt."

"What'd you tell her?" *Please say you did not give her an answer under four words.*

"I said your dad's dead and your mom's a nutcase."

"Oh, great, that covers it all!" My sarcasm flew right over his head, so I tried the direct approach. "That's it? That's all you told her?"

"Pretty cut and dried, ain't it?"

"No, Chad, it's *not cut and dried.*"

"Is to me," he said, and swigged his beer. "She acted strange after I told her though…"

"That's because she thinks there's something wrong with me." Turning away from him, I watched out the passenger window, without saying a word, as the last of Tennessee disappeared.

"Now don't get your panties all in a wad. I know Mom's excited about you coming, because she put clean sheets on my bed. And she's making pot roast with new potatoes and carrots for dinner. She only makes pot roast for special people. Besides, you'll have plenty of time to tell her all about your life after we get married. She'll be like your mom too."

I kept my face turned to the window. Chad pressed his cold beer against the side of my neck. "Quit!" I snapped.

"Still love me?" he asked.

I looked over at him. One side of his mouth was turned up, mischievously. He winked an eye with unfairly long, black eyelashes. "I guess so." As stingy as he was with his words, I decided it was probably best he hadn't told his mom anything more. I would tell her when I got to know her. I would explain everything.

"You sure are sexy when you're pissed," Chad said. Although I tried, I couldn't keep a grin from taking control of my face.

For the rest of the trip, I thought about his mom. I pictured her as having beautiful dark features, like Chad's, and baking pies in a kitchen decorated in rustic country. I liked the idea of having a mother-in-law and a family to call my own. Marrying Chad was the right decision. I was sure of it.

Chad lived in a rural area right outside of Sullivan where nothing but miles of bumpy, wooded land separated each farmhouse. As we pulled the sloped driveway up to his house, I took in my new surroundings. The large hill of a yard, lined with honeysuckle and blackberry bushes, lead to a white aluminum-sided bungalow with black shutters. As we got closer, I saw English ivy growing up the front of the house, and potted mums in terra cotta pots by

the porch. *A good sign,* I thought. *Nice people have flowers.*
As we got out of the car, a grayish Shepard mix, trotted
from around the back. *Nice people have dogs too.*

"Hey there, buddy," Chad said, scratching the dog
behind one ear. "Did you miss me?"

How adorable; he's a dog lover! "What's his name?" I
asked.

"Wolfman," he said. "C'mon, let's go in. Hope Mom's
got dinner ready. I'm starved." He grabbed my wrist and
led me to the back of the house. As we walked, I combed
through my feathered hair with my fingers, and then bent
over and smoothed out the creases in the lap of my jeans.

Chad opened a sliding glass door, and we entered
the eating area of the kitchen. As soon as we went in, a
large dining table was right there. Literally, right there.
We had to squeeze between it and the door just to get in.
There were only four people living in the house and yet
the dining table could have easily accommodated fifteen.
And there were thirteen plates set out. *Who else is coming?*
I wondered.

From what I could see, the house was smaller than
it had appeared from the outside. The kitchen was dark,
the air—close and cigarette-smoky. Contrary to what I'd
expected, there was no one waiting to greet us. But a
heart-shaped plaque that read *welcome* hung on the wall
by the door.

Chad continued on through the house, and I followed
him down a dark wood paneled hallway to the living
room. I saw his father first—a small, weathered man with
a flat face and ruddy skin, kicked back in a worn recliner,

puffing on a cigarette. He glanced at us when we entered the room as if we were a distraction, and then went back to watching TV.

A young woman with big, bouffant hair, who I guessed to be Chad's sister, Trudy, sat board-like on the edge of the sofa. "There they are," she said, in a tone that sounded neither pleased nor surprised, her generous hairdo bouncing like a bobble-head doll's.

In a far corner of the room, Chad's mother—or who I assumed was his mother—filled an overstuffed chair with layers of fat. She looked nothing like I'd imagined. She had unkempt salt and pepper hair, and she was wearing a nearly transparent housedress without a bra, her breasts supported only by her protruding stomach. "You're late," she said. "I've been holding dinner."

Chad put his arm around me. "It took this one longer than I expected to pack."

"I don't have a lot of room for your stuff," his mom said, looking straight at me.

"Oh, that's okay. I can keep some of it in the trunk of Chad's car."

"Whatever." She struggled to get out of the chair. "Now let's eat before my roast dries out."

When both Chad's parents were standing, I couldn't help but notice they were an odd couple. When I first saw his dad, I could tell he was short in stature and small-boned like Chad, because he sat low in his chair, but when he stood, I was startled to see he was barely over five feet tall. His mother, in contrast, was well over five feet seven inches, and significantly overweight. If you examined her face closely, you could see the beautiful woman she once had been, but with age had let herself go. Chad had gotten his deep chocolate eyes and pore-less skin from her.

As Chad's mother led the way back to the kitchen, I tugged at his arm and stopped him in the hallway. "Aren't you going to introduce me?"

"There ain't any need for formal introduction. They know who you are."

"Well, I don't know who *they* are. You haven't even told me their names!"

"Oh. Mom's name is Bobbi, short for Barbara, and Dad's is Chad, like mine, only Mom calls him Big Chad so we'll know which one of us she's talking to."

"*Big* Chad?" I snickered. "It's meant to be a joke, right, like nicknaming a linebacker Tiny?"

Chad was not smiling. "No. Dad's real sensitive about his size. I wouldn't joke about it in front of him if I was you." *Ah, the little man complex. That's where Chad got it.*

"So does your mom call you Little Chad then?"

"Hell no!" He jerked his arm away from my hold. "They call me Chad Jr. Now can we eat?"

In the kitchen, everyone shuffled sideways trying to squeeze in around the massive table. "You can sit anywhere," Bobbi said. "Except there at the head; that's where Big Chad sits." I took Chad's advice and held my giggle inside.

Bobbi began barking orders as she pulled drinking glasses from a cabinet. "Chad Jr., we're going to need one more chair; grab a fold out from the hall closet. Trudy, you get on the phone and call Brenda. Tell her I'm filling bowls now."

"What about Lilly," Chad hollered out from the hall.

"She called right before ya'll walked in," Bobbi hollered back. "Said she was on her way."

Nobody bothered to explain who Brenda and Lilly were, and I was embarrassed to ask, because I didn't want them to know Chad hadn't already told me. But my guess was they were two of his sisters. And judging by the thirteen place settings, either they were both married and had two kids a piece, or they were single mothers, each with three kids. Or one of them had three kids, and the other had one. Or, maybe one of them was single with four kids and the other was childless. These trivial rambling thoughts eased my nerves and busied my mind as I sat awkwardly in my strange new world.

After Chad had set up the extra chair, he took the seat beside me. I leaned in to him and whispered in his ear, "Who's Brenda and Lilly?"

"My sisters. Lilly lives down the road and Brenda's next door. They'll be here in less than five minutes."

Bobbi began placing on the table, bowls filled with new potatoes and carrots in meat juice, macaroni and cheese, and green beans. In another trip, she brought white bread stacked high on a small saucer and a plate of sliced onions. "Can I do anything to help?" I asked.

"No, I think I've got it under control," she said, placing, on the table in front of me, the biggest platter of pulled pork I'd ever seen. Bobbi seemed like the kind of woman who didn't want anyone messing around in her kitchen. The kind of woman who claimed it as her territory and took credit for everything that came out of it. "Thanks anyway," she muttered, as she headed back to the stove.

Two fair-haired toddler boys, close to the same age, appeared at the sliding glass door. A pretty, petite blond and a man in a John Deer cap with lots of scraggly facial hair, were close behind. "Lilly's here," announced Trudy.

Minutes later, another petite woman came to the door. This one had long, brown hair. With her were two older children, a boy and a girl; her husband also had a beard and wore a cap.

When the kids barreled in chattering, suddenly the house was infused with light and life. The two men spoke to me; one of them tipping the bill of his cap. The sisters barely looked my way before they got busy loading their kids' plates with mac and cheese.

No one in Chad's family paid any attention to me, even though I was the elephant in the room. The elephant that was going to marry their son, their brother. The elephant moving in that night. Maybe they were ignoring me because, to them, I was just some kid Chad had brought home and they were only tolerating my presence for him. Maybe they were too busy getting ready to eat to be bothered—a hungry family that appreciated their meals. When things calmed down and everyone was seated at the table, the questions would begin, and all eyes would turn to me. Or, although not probable, they were ignoring me because Chad had already talked to them about me, talked their heads off about how he adored me, talked so much they felt like they knew me and I was already part of the family.

After we had filled our plates, I braced myself for the interrogation to come. But no one asked me a single question; no one addressed me at all. They talked around me about the best way to get the wild taste out of deer meat, and debated who had really won the corn-hole championship last summer. In one way, I was relieved nobody asked me any uncomfortable questions, and in another way, being disregarded by them hurt my feelings.

When the meat platter had been reduced by three-fourths, and the mac and cheese bowl was empty, someone finally acknowledged I was there. "So when ya'll getting married, Tuesday?" Lilly asked.

Before I had a chance to answer, Bobbi interjected, "Better be quick because ya'll ain't sleeping in a bed together until you do."

"Oh, Mom, we ain't gonna do nothing." Chad lied. There had yet to come a day when we were together that he hadn't tried to nail me.

"I *know* you're not because I ain't giving you the chance," Bobbi said.

Lilly's husband glanced up from his plate, smiled sleazily at Chad, and said, "I know somebody who's gonna be making a trip to Illinois real soon."

"You're damn straight," Chad said. "I think I'll take a personal day tomorrow."

Everyone looked at me and laughed. My face was hot. I didn't have to see it to know it was glowing like a stoplight.

MR. AND MRS. CHICKEN

EARLY THE NEXT morning, Chad and I went to Shawneetown, Illinois and got a marriage license. The county clerk told us there was a chapel down the road where a minister may be able to perform the ceremony. He offered to make an appointment for us to get married the following day, after our twenty-four hour waiting period was up.

On the way home, we stopped at the only jewelry store in Sullivan, and Chad bought the cheapest wedding bands they had. We were back at his parents' house in time for lunch. Again, the entire family was there. The large kitchen table was starting to make sense. The Sutton togetherness made me uneasy, and yet I found it to be endearing, and couldn't wait to be a part it. This almost unfathomable promise of having a family drew me to Chad even more.

Lilly and Brenda had finished eating and were lighting cigarettes. Everyone in Chad's family smoked except for Bobbi. Theirs was a nervous, frantic habit. They fired up the first cigarette of the morning with shaky hands, and then throughout the day they lit one after the other—sometimes one *off* of the other. From across the table, through the veil of smoke in the room, Bobbi eyed me as she chewed on a toothpick. "So why ain't you living with your mother?"

"She doesn't want me to." I slid a cigarette from Chad's pack and lit it up. Usually I only smoked while drinking with my friends, but the impending conversation called for a cigarette.

"What did you do to make her mad?"

"I didn't do anything. She's hated me ever since I was little. She abused me."

"I don't believe in all that abuse horseshit. Kids don't want to do what they're told, and then they holler abuse when their parents try to teach them right from wrong." Bobbi plucked the toothpick from her mouth and threw it into her empty plate. "And she don't hate you either; there ain't a mother alive that hates her kid. You should tell her you're sorry."

"Sorry for what?"

"For whatever you did to make her kick you out."

Chad broke in. "Mom, Tuesday doesn't have to make up with her mama if she doesn't want to. That's her business."

"Well... I suppose it is. But that don't make it right. Kids should respect their parents; we do the best we can."

After supper, Chad and I went for a drive to get some "alone time," as he put it to his parents. I knew he really wanted to get laid. But I wasn't in the mood. As soon as we were in the car, I asked him why his mother didn't like me.

"Oh don't mind her. She's real protective of us kids, that's all. She didn't like any of the in-laws in the beginning. Don't worry she'll come around."

He was right; she would come around. After all, I would soon be her daughter-in-law. She had to like me, didn't she?

When we pulled up to the chapel the next morning, I began to get jittery for the first time. Up until that point, the whole marriage business had seemed like a game—a game of chicken—between Chad and me, like two children, each stubbornly waiting for the other to back out.

Everything had happened in a blur. I met Chad at the liquor store. He told me he loved me. We agreed to get married because he was tired of driving back and forth between Sullivan and Nashville, and I needed somewhere to go when Aunt Macy started her new life with Edwin. We ate with his family three times, bought a marriage license and rings, and now there we were at the chapel getting ready to seal the deal. Or—as Chad had told one of his friends over the phone the night before—seal our coffins.

After Chad parked the car, we sat outside the chapel for a few minutes staring at the door while he finished a cigarette. We were taking our game of chicken to the limit. *This is it*, I thought. *This is where he calls the whole thing off. We will return the rings and I'll go begging back to Aunt Macy…*

"Are we going in, or are we gonna sit here and watch the leaves blow by?" Trudy said from the backseat. I'd forgotten she was back there. We'd asked her to come with us to act as a witness. She was between jobs and didn't have anything better to do, so she agreed.

Chad and I opened our doors and got out of the car at exactly the same time. I had on a pale yellow shift dress Aunt Macy had made for me. It was the closest to white of all the dresses I owned. He was wearing jeans and a blue button down shirt Bobbi had ironed for him before we left. Trudy was the most dressed up of the three of us, in a tight, black skirt and a ruffled white blouse. She had perfectly smooth hair, like a big platinum helmet, curled under on one side, flipped up on the other—a style much older than she was.

We marched in single file up to the chapel—Chad, me, and then Trudy, who struggled to walk through the gravel in spike heels. The orderliness of our movements was a stark contrast to the collage of chaos floating around in my head: Aunt Macy's crying face, ball-peen hammers, and Bobbi chewing on a toothpick, shooting accusatory expressions my way.

When we got to the entrance of the chapel, I adjusted my dress and fluffed my hair. Chad put his hand on the door handle and then turned around. "Do we just go in?"

I didn't know, so I looked behind me, at Trudy. "Of course we go in," she said. "It's a church for Christ sake. Anybody can go in."

Inside, an older, scruffy-bearded man in a faded black suit walked up to greet us. "Reverend Templeton," he said, shaking Chad's hand loosely. "And I'm guessing your name is Chad, and you're here to marry one of these lovely girls."

Chad pointed at me. "This one. The other one's my sister."

"Got your license and rings?" asked Reverend Templeton.

"Yep" Chad had my ring on his pinky, and I had his on my thumb. He pulled the folded marriage license from his back pocket and handed it to the reverend.

"And I see you brought a witness." Reverend Templeton nodded at Trudy. "Looks like everything's in order. Shall we get started?"

Rigidly positioned beside Chad—both of us in front of the reverend—I scanned the empty pews for Aunt Macy, even though she'd told me she wouldn't come when I called her the night before. I hoped somehow she'd changed her mind. Naturally I thought of Mama. I didn't want her to be there, but I needed her to be there, or the idea of her. I thought of Daddy too, and the weddings I'd seen in the movies where teary-eyed fathers walked their daughters down the aisle to give them away to become wives. *What would Daddy think of Chad, a man who couldn't have been any more opposite from him?* Not long before his wreck, he had given me some advice about choosing a husband. "Be sure the man you marry makes you feel good about yourself," he'd said. Now, three years later, I wondered if I had made the right choice.

After a couple of *I do's,* it was all over, or, depending on perception, had just begun. We stopped at a liquor store on the way back to Sullivan and Trudy bought us a bottle of champagne to celebrate. Chad talked her into filling his cooler with beer too. We had supper with the family and not one person congratulated us. After we'd eaten, Chad and I changed clothes to go out partying with his friends, which meant driving out to some secluded place in the country and getting drunk, maybe smoking a joint.

Chad chose a spot not far from his house for the party. On the ground, in a grassy area, he spread a blanket he'd swiped from his bed, and then brought out a Coleman lantern, and the cooler of beer. His friends all showed up in one car. One of them brought a jam box, which he turned up to the max. It was a cool night, but not too cool for us to sit outside in our hoodies. We all plopped down on the blanket and started drinking.

After almost two hours, we were pretty well lit. A guy named Troy, who was invited only because he supplied the pot, rolled a fat joint and passed it around. I didn't care for pot. The last time I'd smoked it with Sheila, I became so dizzy I had to crawl over to some bushes and throw up chunks of Big Mac, so when it was my turn to take a draw, I waved it off.

Since I was the only girl there, I was getting a lot of attention. The more liquored-up everyone got, the friendlier they became, especially Troy. He sat close beside me, and every time I emptied a can of beer, he got me another one. Under the influence of alcohol, I didn't notice Chad fuming on the other side of me until suddenly he sprang up "Hey motherfucker, you *do* see that ring on her finger, don't you?"

Troy stood facing Chad. "Yeah, I see it. What about it?"

An image of the ball-peen hammer popped into my head. I jumped to my feet. "Chad, please don't fight!" I begged, pulling at his arm.

"You stay out of this," he said, shoving me aside.

I squeezed in between him and Troy. "Please, Chad, you're embarrassing me!" He shoved me aside again, this time hard enough for me to fall.

In the movies, when a girl gets pushed down by a guy, she whimpers and holds whatever body part that got hurt. Not me. I got up, charging like a bull, and pushed Chad back, and down into the gravel road. Next thing I knew we were rolling around on the ground. Chad and I were close to the same height, but he probably outweighed me by a few pounds. I knew I was strong, stronger than most girls, due to all the strenuous work I had to do as a kid, but while we were wrestling, my strength astounded even me. At one point, I actually thought I could beat him up, however I soon found out I couldn't, because he was much stronger. He overpowered and straddled me, and then pinned both my wrists above my head. I could feel the gravel digging into my forearms. I bucked my hips and threw him off of me enough to where I could squirm out of his hold. When I went for him again, one of his friends pulled me off.

"What the fuck!" Chad yelled, as he got up and

brushed himself off. "Are you crazy trying to fight me like a man? He started half-laughing, acting like he hadn't been serious while we were fighting, like he'd let up on me because I was a girl. His friends laughed nervously with him. "I could kill you if I wanted to!"

"Nobody's ever gonna hit me again!" I screamed.

"I didn't hit you!"

"You pushed me down—same thing!"

He stood staring at me for a second or two before the light in his head switched on. "Oh yeah, I forgot; your mama beat on you when you were a kid, so now you think everybody's gonna beat you." He started walking toward me. "Come here, baby," he said. "I'm sorry."

I dodged away from him. "Just don't ever hit me again!"

"I'm not gonna hurt you ever again, I promise."

Everyone else was getting their stuff together to leave. It was time for Chad and me to go home too.

That night, with Bobbi's permission, Chad and I slept in a bed together for the first time. We had mandatory wedding night sex, and then turned our backs to each other. As I drifted off to sleep, I thought about what had happened earlier. There were two things I'd learned from my fight with Chad. One, I was no longer a victim, because if anybody ever hit me I would fight back. And two, Chad and I both were a little bit crazy.

LITTLE MAN, BIG GUN

THE DAYS WERE long while Chad was at work, sitting in a dreary house with Bobbi watching soap operas and game shows on TV. After I made the bed and took a shower, there was nothing else to do. Chad told me his 442 was parked in the driveway if I needed to go somewhere, but there wasn't any reason to get out. I had no friends there, and I was broke, except for twenty dollars from my last paycheck.

When Big Chad changed to second shift at the mine, I was glad, hoping his presence would buffer the awkwardness of Bobbi and me spending our days together in silence. But like his son, Big Chad was a man of few words. Now there were three of us in the house not talking.

A couple of weeks after Chad and I moved in, Bobbi came barging in our room in the middle of the night and flipped on the overhead light. She was in a tizzy. "Chad Jr. did you see your daddy at the mine today?"

Chad squinted in the light that flooded the room. "No, I didn't see him."

"Are you in such a hurry to get home these days that you can't even bother to look for your daddy?"

"Sometimes I see him going in as I'm coming out, but sometimes I don't. He was probably somewhere smoking with his cronies. Why you wanna know?"

"Cause it's going on one o'clock in the morning and he ain't home yet."

Chad sprung up and stepped into some jeans that were draped over a chair by the bed.

"What does this mean," I asked Chad.

"It means Dad's out on a drunk, that's what."

Chad and Bobbi rushed into the kitchen, and I followed. Trudy called the hospital to see if Big Chad was there. Then she tried the jail. After both places were ruled out, Chad grabbed his car keys and said he was going to the bars to look for his dad.

"I'm going too," I said.

"Oh no you're not. These bars ain't no place for a woman."

Half an hour later, Chad came back and told us he saw his dad's car at the Hot Spot, a seedy night club right outside of Uniontown. "The Hot Spot closes at three o'clock," he said. "After that, he'll either come home or hang out at some other drunk's house."

"Thank you Chad Jr.," Bobbi said, wearily. "Guess all we can do now is wait."

"I'm going back to bed, or I won't be fit for work tomorrow," said Chad. "Come on, Tuesday."

Seemed like we had no more than dozed off, when I heard the bedroom door squeak like it always did when somebody opened it. The sound of heavy footsteps followed the squeak. In the dark, I could barely see the outline of Big Chad's diminutive body standing by Chad's side of the bed. He had something in his hand, but I couldn't make out what it was. "This is my goddamn house," he said, in a raspy voice.

Chad stirred. I turned on the light beside the bed and saw the object Big Chad held in his hand was a gun—and it was now aimed at Chad.

"I know it's your house, Dad," Chad said.

"Who in the hell do you people think you are coming in my house sleeping in my bed and eating my food?" He cut his eyes over at me.

"I'm your son, Dad, and Tuesday's my wife. Remember we got married?"

By this time, Bobbi, who must have fallen asleep on the sofa, had entered the room. Trudy popped in behind her. "Big Chad, what are you doing?" Bobbi asked.

Big Chad aimed the gun at Bobbi. "You better get your fat ass outta here before I shoot you too!"

"Put that gun away!" demanded Bobbi. "That's your son!"

"He ain't my son; he don't look a thing like me! He looks like a damn chink!"

Bobbi took a step forward. "Please put that away before you hurt somebody."

Big Chad raised the gun and pointed it at Bobbi's face. "I'll shoot you!" He made a sweeping motion with the gun "I'll shoot you all! I'll shoot who I damn well please because this is *my* house!" He directed the gun at Chad again. "Get your scrawny ass up out of my bed and come with me to the kitchen; I wanna talk to you."

Chad, wearing nothing but his underwear, got up out of bed and walked to the kitchen with Big Chad holding the gun to the back of his head. The rest of us followed.

"Come on, Big Chad, put the gun down," Bobbi pleaded again. "Let me fix you some breakfast."

"I ain't hungry, and if you tell me to put this gun down one more time I'm shooting *somebody*."

We all sat down at the table. Using his free hand, Big Chad pulled a cigarette from a crushed pack of non-filtered Camel's in his shirt pocket. As he went to light it, he got a piece of tobacco on his tongue and spit it into the air. Everyone at the table jumped. He took a long drag from the cigarette and blew the smoke up above his head. "Now, here's the problem," he began, eyeballing Chad. "You say you're my son but I don't believe you. I'm gonna need you to prove it."

"Prove it?" Chad asked. "How am I supposed to do that?"

Bobbi cut in again, "You know he's yours..."

"I thought I told you to shut up!" snapped Big Chad. Then he turned his bloodshot eyes back to the matter at hand.

"He's short like you," Trudy offered.

"That ain't provin' nothin'. Chinks are short like me too."

Trudy tried another approach. "Hey Daddy, Hot Spot will be open again here in a few minutes. Let's you and me go down there and get us a drink."

"Yeah, that's a good idea; we'll do that as soon as I finish up here."

This went on for about half an hour. Big Chad saying my Chad wasn't his son. My Chad saying he didn't know how to prove it, and Bobbi and Trudy cutting in regularly trying to help, but only making matters worse. The word *shoot* was thrown around a lot and so was *kill*, but I didn't think for a minute anybody was going to get shot, let alone killed. To me, it seemed like I was sitting in the middle of a bad play with a bunch of people who were overacting.

Eventually Big Chad got tired of holding the gun and put it on the table in front of him. As the alcohol began to wear off, I saw reality dawn in his eyes. A while longer, and he nodded off, his cigarette with its long, curling ash burning dangerously close to his fingers. Seeing his chance, Chad grabbed the gun while Bobbi and Trudy helped Big Chad to bed.

By this time, morning had slipped in, and it was too late for Chad to go to work. Bobbi called in a sick day for him and one for Big Chad too. For the rest of the morning, everybody sat around smoking and discussing the events of the night before.

When Chad and I had a minute alone, I asked him what a chink was and he told me it was a slang word for a person of Asian descent. Actually he said it was a Japanese dude, but I knew what he meant.

"Why would your dad think you were a chink? You don't even look Asian."

"He thinks everybody's a chink when he's drunk. He fought in the Korean War, and I think he gets flashbacks sometimes."

I could tell from the family's reaction that what had happened was not an isolated incident. Knowing this, helped me to gain a better understanding of Chad's family, of why they were so tight, and why the grown kids spent so much time at their parents' house. I could also see why Bobbi was so protective of them. As children, when Big Chad "went on a drunk" and became violent, they had clung to Bobbi for safety. Now they were still afraid, still clinging to her emotionally, and finding it difficult to break away.

As hard as Chad had tried to conceal his fear, I'd seen it on his face as his dad held the gun to his head. He was not as tough as he would've liked for everyone to believe. My heart ached at the thought of Chad having to deal with such trauma as a young boy. That day, I loved my husband a little more.

THE VIRUS

B IG CHAD DIDN'T scare me, but I let on like he did, and used my feigned fear as leverage to try to get Chad to move out sooner. It must have worked, because a couple of days after Big Chad's drunk Chad asked Bobbi to front him the money to buy a trailer. He promised to pay her back when he got his income tax return.

Chad already had in mind the trailer he was going to buy for us. His sister, Lilly, was selling hers, so she and her husband could move into a house. However she was renting the land the trailer was on, so we would have to move it somewhere else. Chad had that figured out too. He'd made a deal with his Mom and Dad to put the trailer on the lot behind their house. Living behind Bobbi and Big Chad was not exactly what I had in mind when I asked Chad if we could move out of his parents' house, but it was better than the alternative, and the arrangement was all we could afford at the time. The good news was we wouldn't have to move the trailer very far because Lilly lived less than a mile away.

Within a week, we'd bought the trailer and Chad had arranged to have it moved. The guys he hired to move it had some difficulty pulling up the steep hill behind his parents' house. Once I held my breath because the trailer almost toppled over, but somehow, between Chad and his brothers-in-law, they managed to get it set up, anchored and underpinned, all in one day.

Trailers had always been baffling to me. I'd never even seen one until our family moved from Tennessee to Kentucky when I was around twelve. I couldn't make sense of why a house would need wheels unless its owners moved around a lot. From what I'd seen in Kentucky, once people got their trailers set up and underpinned they pretty much stayed put. In our case, I was glad our house had wheels, because if I had anything to do with it, we wouldn't be living behind Chad's parents for long.

All the appliances, including a washer and dryer, came with the trailer. Lilly let the curtains go too, and she even threw in her old sofa. Chad brought his television set and full-size bed from his room. We scraped together the money to buy a yard sale dinette, and Bobbi gave us a couple of pictures to hang on the walls. It would take some time to get settled in and comfortable, but we were off to a good start.

The trailer was old and outdated, and a faded chartreuse color, but I was happy Chad and I had a place to call our own. The day we bought our new home, I made a vow to always take good care of it. Each day I would clean until everything sparkled, decorate the rooms, and have dinner on the table when Chad got home from work. Our life was going to be perfect.

The first night in our new home *was* perfect. We sat on the orange shag carpeted floor of the living room and ate our dinner of cheese sandwiches and pretzels by candlelight, and drank Boone's Farm Strawberry Hill straight from the bottle. We were both too exhausted from the move to talk and chew our food too, but in between bites we passed cheesy smiles back and forth between us. We had no need for words, and there were none to describe how ecstatic we were. Chad had to go in to work the next day, so after we ate, we crawled to *our* mattress on *our* floor, and passed out in each other's arms.

For a few weeks after we moved into the trailer, I busied myself with cleaning. There was a film of cigarette smoke on the windows and walls that took lots of Spic-n-Span and elbow grease to cut through. The curtains smelled of smoke, so I took them all down, washed them by hand, and then hung them over the shower rod in the bathroom to dry. Every morning I prepared Chad's lunch bucket for work, and in the evenings I made our dinner. He didn't seem to like my cooking as much as he did his mom's, though. I could tell because he insisted we eat at her house three or four times a week.

It didn't take long for our new home to change from the love nest I was trying to create to a gathering place for Chad and his friends to drink and smoke pot. At first, I tried to play happy hostess, to fetch our guests' beers when they needed them, empty overflowing ashtrays, and keep the chip bowls filled. But after a while, the nonstop party got old, and when a new film of smoke coated the windows and walls, I realized all the cleaning I had done was for nothing. When I protested, Chad made it clear he was paying for the trailer and his friends were always welcome, and unless I wanted to be out on the streets I'd better keep my mouth shut.

If Chad threw me out, I knew I could move in with Aunt Macy and Edwin. But I didn't want to, because then I'd have to admit to them my marriage had failed. Besides, I liked living on my own, having a place, being a wife, and I was content with my new life for the most part. I had plenty to eat, and Chad didn't beat me or lock me in a room, and he only talked mean to me when he was mad, or drunk, or both. Everything was fine as long as I went along with whatever he wanted. So I sucked up my discontentment with a smile, tapped into the high tolerance I'd developed as a child, and went on living.

Just over a month after Chad and I were married, I caught a nasty stomach virus. Everything I ate came right back up. When the virus persisted for more than a few days, Bobbi pronounced me pregnant. *There's no way I could be pregnant*, I thought. Most of the time Chad and I were careful, as careful as two young newlyweds with raging hormones could be. I ignored Bobbi's nonsense and went on for another week, throwing up every day, telling myself and everyone else I had a virus.

When Chad's shift at the mine changed to seconds, he took me to the doctor, who confirmed what I'd been trying so hard to deny: my virus was actually a four week old fetus. When the doctor passed on the results of the test, the truth slapped me in the face—I was going to be a mother. *Mother? Mother!* The mere thought of the word evoked nothing but negative reactions from me.

The news of my pregnancy mortified me, but I didn't let my true emotions show. I pretended to be the joyful, expectant mother, while inside I questioned my ability to take on such a role. Chad, on the other hand, was tickled when I told him. Getting me pregnant played right along with his never-ending quest to prove he was a man. A big man. A strong man. A virile man. "Yeah, I've already knocked up my old lady," he would say to his friends in between tokes. He couldn't wait to get back home to tell the family. I wondered how Bobbi would react when she found out she was stuck with me.

To my surprise, the family welcomed my pregnancy with open arms. Brenda and Lilly dug out some of their old maternity clothes and brought them to me. Everyone was chatty and attentive. Even Big Chad started smoking his cigarettes in a room away from me. Their enthusiasm was catchy, and soon I found myself filing through baby names in my head, and mentally turning the spare bedroom of the trailer into a nursery.

Home alone that evening, after Chad left for work, I started thinking. Funny how I, of all people, hadn't given any thought to having kids, as if being a mother wasn't even an option for me. Chad and I had never discussed becoming parents. But then we never discussed much of anything. That was the Sutton way. They let stuff happen and then dealt with the fallout.

Most days I tried not to think about the possibility that I could have inherited my mother's legacy of abuse. And most days I didn't, because I was so physically ill I could think of nothing but my illness. For the first six months, I threw up every morning, starting with my prenatal vitamin. Throughout the day, I threw up whenever I tried to eat, or when I came in contact with certain smells that turned my stomach, like the mustiness of coal on Chad's clothes, and the green apple scented shampoo he used to wash his hair. And cigarette smoke, and ashtrays, and coffee, and the list went on and on. Even when my stomach was empty of food, when I smelled these things I threw up bile, and then when I'd emptied my stomach of bile, I dry heaved until my insides were in my throat. Sometimes I threw up for no apparent reason, as if my mind were punishing my body for getting pregnant without its consent. My doctor said he'd never seen such a relentless case of morning sickness. The only foods I could keep down were crackers and Popsicles, so that's what I lived on for the first few months.

When I wasn't vomiting I was sleeping. To escape my reality, I surrendered to sleep's soothing otherworld far more often than I should have. Locked in the trailer, curtains drawn, I sometimes slept for fifteen hours straight. But when I began having disturbing nightmares about becoming a mother, even sleep was no longer a safe haven. One dream was particularly frightening and persistent:

*I am in a hospital room, sitting up in a bed with pil-
lows propped behind me. A nurse walks in cradling an infant
wrapped in a pink blanket. As she brings the baby closer, I can
see a downy head and tiny flailing arms, hear soft gurgling
sounds, but as hard as I try, I can't see the baby's face, only a
blurry, blank spot where a face should be. "Take her away!" I
scream when I see my baby has no face.*

*"You don't want your own baby?" the nurse asks. "I know
why you don't want her; it's because she's ugly like you!" When
I look up at the nurse I see she is my mother.*

The family became concerned because I was dropping weight at such a rapid rate, but I wasn't too worried because, although the rest of my body was getting
thin, my belly was steadily growing, and I could feel the
life inside of me getting stronger every day. When I went
for my check-up, the doctor assured me that somehow,
despite my inability to hold down anything of nutritional
value, the baby was developing normally.

Toward the end of my pregnancy, my morning sickness began to subside enough for me to pick up weight,
but the nausea never went away completely. I reached the
point where I wanted the baby to be born so I would stop
being sick, but at the same time, I dreaded its arrival. At
least while my baby was inside of me I knew it would be
safe.

Early May, Aunt Macy called to say she and Edwin were
going to Florida to get married and then taking a cruise
for their honeymoon. She wasn't happy when I'd finally

gotten up the courage a few months earlier to call and tell her about my pregnancy. She knew a baby would kill the chance of me going back to college in the near future. But being the classy lady she was, she never showed her disappointment to me. I had sent her an invitation to a baby shower Bobbi and the sisters were giving me, but she was going to be on her honeymoon then. She apologized that she would not be able to come, but promised to send a gift in the mail.

We had the baby shower at Bobbi's house, as planned. The gathering was informal, with Styrofoam bowls of nuts and pastel mints, and plates of store-bought cookies. Middle-aged women in mom jeans and stretch pants trailed in with huge packages of disposable diapers and boxed infant sleeping gowns in tow. One woman had a yellow plastic tub filled with bottles of oil, lotion and shampoo. Another one, with a bad home perm, seemed to be particularly concerned with the proper cleaning of the baby's orifices. She provided what looked like a year's supply of Q-tips, and a nose suctioning device resembling a small turkey baster that I was sure I wouldn't be able to figure out how to use. I didn't know hardly anyone at the shower, and I had a funny feeling I could have stayed home and no one would have missed me.

My doctor could not tell the sex of the baby from the sonogram. Chad had made it known he wanted a boy. In his family of many "split-tails," male children were coveted. During the last month of my pregnancy, I found myself also secretly hoping we would have a boy, but for my own reasons. I remembered Mama saying over and over that she hated me because I was a girl and because I was ugly. I thought maybe the curse of abuse in my family was for females only. This theory made sense because she never touched my brothers. I decided if the baby came out a boy I would be safe. I stopped picking out girl's names.

As my due date neared, Bobbi began trolling the yard sales for baby items. She brought home stacks of slightly-worn unisex onesies, and some equipment the baby wouldn't need for months: a walker, a playpen and a springy jump-chair thing. The trailer looked like a ghetto day care center. When I protested, she said, "I've had six kids; trust me, you'll need these things soon enough."

June 27th, I went into labor around midnight. Chad, Bobbi, Trudy, Brenda and Lilly were huddled around me at the hospital, but even with all the support, something was missing. *Someone* was missing. I had stuck by my word and not contacted Mama since that day in the restaurant. I'd been so busy I hadn't even thought of her.

If my mind was indeed trying to punish me for becoming pregnant, it wasn't done with me yet. Twenty hours into labor, I hadn't fully dilated. At eleven-thirty the following night, after more than twenty-three hours of hard labor and intermittent vomiting, the doctor had to take the baby with forceps. It was a girl.

The nurse prepared my baby for me to hold. I watched, terrified, as if she were about to hand me a giant scorpion. Like in my nightmare, I could see the baby's arms flailing and hear her gentle throaty sounds. When the nurse lowered her into my arms, cocooned in a white blanket, I held my breath and looked down. *She has a face; a perfect face!*

Babies are not particularly beautiful when they're first born, all pink and puckered from being in water too long. It's the *idea* of them that's beautiful, their purity, their innocence, the awareness that they are part of you. In that sense my baby was beautiful. In reality, she had blotchy skin, her eyes were bulbous, and she slightly resembled a chink. I worried how she would be received by Big Chad the next time he threw a drunk.

As soon as I felt the warmth of my daughter's body against mine, my love was instant and undeniable, and my instinct to nurture and protect her overwhelmed me. All at once, she became my everything. The doll I was never allowed to have as a child. The unconditional love I'd always longed for. My second chance at happiness. All this was a heavy load for such a fragile creature to carry. A knot rose in the back of my throat... and I began to cry. I pressed my lips to her forehead and whispered, "We're going to be okay."

BECOMING OUR PARENTS

B ECAUSE CHAD AND I had been so intent on the
baby being a boy, we had no girl's names selected.
Chad hurried down to the hospital gift shop and bought a
book of baby names. After much deliberation and debate,
we decided on Molly, and for her middle name, we went
with Leigh, like mine. Molly Leigh, a name with a ring. It
rolled off the tongue. I loved it.

Chad had hoped for a boy and so had his dad.
"Another split-tail," Big Chad quipped. "You'll have a
half-dozen more before you get a boy." *Not me,* I thought.
If Chad and I were lucky enough to be halfway decent
parents to one kid, with our families' history of dysfunction, we had no business tempting fate again.

Because I'd dropped so much weight during my pregnancy and labor, I went home from the hospital in some
jeans and a tee-shirt I'd worn before I became pregnant.
Bobbi had bought Molly a cute pink gown and matching
cap to wear. Chad had the car warmed up and ready for

Molly and me. He even opened the door and helped us in. He was the proud father doing everything right.

The family had set up the bassinette, handed down from Lilly, in our bedroom in the trailer, and gathered everything we would need to care for Molly. Thanks to the baby shower, we had plenty of diapers and wipes and lotions. Thanks to Bobbi's yard sale finds, Molly wouldn't need clothes for at least four months. All the tools I needed to be a good mother had been provided. The rest was up to me.

Molly was born a girl, but I couldn't imagine how I could ever stop loving her, like Mama had stopped loving me. Still, even with all the love I had to give my baby, I wasn't sure if I was capable of being a good mother to her. Mama's emotional abandonment and ensuing abuse during my formative years had left me with one horrific model for motherhood. All I'd learned from her was what *not* to do, from there I was lost. But I genuinely wanted to be a good parent, so for the first few months, I asked a lot of questions, read books on child rearing, and like most new parents, winged the rest.

What I lacked in experience I tried to make up for with attention and affection. Every time Molly whimpered, I pounced to her side. While Chad was at work, I spent my time dressing her in frilly outfits and taking her picture. When she slept, I was lonely for her. Sometimes I woke her up from her naps because I missed her so much.

Chad began to get jealous of my attention to Molly. One night, after several beers he said, "You give that baby more attention than you ever gave me."

"She needs my attention. You're able to take care of yourself."

"Taking care of her is one thing, but you're obsessed!"

"Maybe I am, but you're jealous of a baby, and that's sick!"

"I'm not jealous! I just think you should remember you have a husband too!"

By his standards, I *had* been neglecting him. And granted, I did only what was absolutely necessary to fulfill my wifely duties. I made his lunch for work and washed his clothes. I kept the trailer clean, and in the rare occasion we didn't eat at Bobbi's, I cooked for him. When he insisted on sex, I served it up, placing it in front of him like a plate of cold grits. But all this wasn't enough. He had grown accustomed to being the center of my world, to me rushing to meet him at the door when he walked in, hanging on his every word, jumping at his commands, and being willing and ready to do anything with him, from fishing at the stripper pit to mudding on his four-wheeler. But I was a mother now, the most important job of my life, and he and his needs had been forced to the back of the bus.

Chad had begun to drink more, and his trashy drug friends had started coming to the trailer and hanging around till morning. It was a biting cold night in late November. A recent light snow had frozen on the ground. Chad had his friend, Harry, over and they were in the living room drinking. As I usually did when he went on one of his all night partying sprees, I'd taken Molly into our bedroom away from the smoke and blaring stereo, and shut the door. She, now about five months old, was sleeping soundly while I watched TV.

Chad and Harry were unusually quiet that night. The music was turned down and they were speaking in low, secretive voices. I knew they were up to something, so I pressed my ear to the bedroom door and heard Chad talking about visiting a local drug dealer for some Quaaludes. In an instant, I became someone else, someone I recognized. I became my mother. I flung open the bedroom door and stormed down the hall to the living room. The front door to the trailer was open, and Chad had his car keys in hand about to leave. "Where do you think you're going?" I asked.

"Out."

I balled up both my fists. Only once before had I been as angry as I was then. A snapshot from the past flashed back to me as lucid as the day it had happened: *Pain pierces my kidney as Mama rears her foot back to kick me again. Before the blow lands, I jump to my feet and grab her by the wrist. Her soft flesh easily yields under my fingernails. In her eyes I see the dread of what she sees in mine. "My name is Tuesday, Mama!" I scream, as I twist her arm. "Say my name! Say it! Say Tuesday!" She winces from the pain of my grip, and on some sick level, her suffering pleases me, so I squeeze even tighter. "Don't you think you've punished me long enough, Mama? Don't you think I've suffered enough for what I did? I can't take it anymore! I won't take it anymore!"*

Propelled by my rage, without saying a word, I plowed into Chad and pushed him out into the snow, face-first. When Harry went to the door to take a look,

I shoved him out as well. Standing in my nightgown, I watched from the trailer doorway as the two men struggled to their feet. "You dope head bastard!" I screamed, my hot words flying out into the night in white puffs. "You've got a baby in the next room trying to sleep and all you can think about is getting drugs! You're both worthless pieces of shit!"

Harry started laughing, and Chad laughed too—at first. Then, as if a light switch flipped off in his eyes, they went black. For the first time, I became fully conscious of what I'd done and slammed the front door and locked it, and then bolted back into the bedroom and shut that door too.

Chad kicked the front door, once, twice, and on the third kick, it flew open and banged against the wall behind it. I heard his furious feet pounding the floor of the hallway. He kicked the bedroom door open in one try. Startled by the noise, Molly woke up crying. Chad pushed past me, dashed to the closet and grabbed his loaded hunting rifle and aimed it in my direction. Normally I wasn't afraid of Chad, in the same way I wasn't afraid of his dad, but I knew he had it in him to be violent, and I could see in his eyes that I had pushed him over the edge.

Suddenly he changed the direction of the rifle to Molly. "I'm gonna make you watch me shoot your baby and then I'm shootin' you!" he said in an almost demonic voice.

I snatched Molly up from her crib, and holding her tight to my chest, ran in bare feet, through the trailer, outside and down the icy hill toward Bobbi and Big Chad's house.

"You bitch!" Chad yelled, chasing after me. "Come back here!"

When I reached his parents' house, I beat on the sliding glass door with the back of my fist. A light came on, and Bobbi peeked from behind one corner of the curtain.

"Bobbi! Let me in!" I begged. "Chad's going to shoot us!"

Chad stood behind me, the rifle poised against his shoulder. "Mom, don't you dare open that fuckin' door!"

"You ain't gonna shoot nobody," Bobbi said, from behind the curtain. "Now put down the rifle, son. And Tuesday you go on back up to the trailer and get Molly out of the cold!"

Maybe she was right; maybe Chad was like his daddy—all talk, no show. Then I remembered the ball-peen hammer and panicked. I darted away and ran next door to Brenda's trailer and banged on the door. I knew they were home because both cars were there. I banged and banged, but nobody came to let me in.

Slipping Molly under the front of my flannel night-gown to keep her warm, I headed for the street with no idea where I was going. My feet hit the icy pavement like dead meat, and I am eight eight-years-old-again, *barefoot in the snow, naked in the snow, running, running as fast as my scrawny legs will take me. In my hand I'm carrying a single piece of trash, a wad of paper; something Mama insisted had to go outside to the trash barrel right after I'd stripped off my clothes to take a bath.*

"You must take this trash out now!" she'd said, with life or death urgency. "I want it out of here this instant!

I started to cry. "But I'm naked, Mama! Let me put on my clothes first!"

"No, there's no time! Now do as I say before I give you something to cry about!"

The trash barrel is at the far end of the yard. The ground is frozen crunchy, and my feet are prickly, like I'm running on needles. It's freezing; my breath in front of me is thick with frost, but I'm not concerned with the cold. My only worry is that someone will see me, see me naked, and I pray the approaching darkness will clothe me...

Chad pulled up beside me in the car. He leaned over and pushed open the passenger side door. "Get in," he said.

I ignored him, picked up my pace.

"Come on, baby, I'm not going to shoot you. I didn't even bring the rifle."

I stopped and looked over at him. He was telling the truth; he didn't have the rifle, but I remembered the ball-peen hammer under the seat and started walking again.

"I'm not going to hurt you, I promise. Now please get in the car before Molly freezes to death."

Molly was crying, shivering. I couldn't feel my fingers and toes. I had no other choice. I got in the car. He handed me a blanket he'd brought to cover Molly, and a coat and furry house slippers for me to put on. I no longer felt we were threatened. He was back to the reasonable Chad I knew.

"Baby, you know I would never shoot you and Molly.

Come on, cut me some slack! You threw me out in the snow in front of my best friend!"

"Cut you some slack? You said you were going to shoot me, Chad! I can almost understand that after what I did. But Molly? Why would you want to shoot your baby daughter?"

"I lost my head. I didn't know what I was saying. Ain't that what happened to you when you pushed me in the snow? My old man has threatened to shoot his kids hundreds of times, but I don't think he'd really ever do it. People say stuff they don't mean when their mad and drunk."

"If you ever do anything like that again, I'll take Molly and go back to Aunt Macy's," I lied. The truth was I had nowhere to go. I couldn't go back to Aunt Macy's, now—not with a baby. Even if she would have taken me back, I couldn't bring myself to mess up her life with Edwin. She had been too good to me.

Chad loved me and I loved him because he loved me, and because we shared the same wounds from our dysfunctional childhoods. He was a decent man battling demons the same way I was. Once I had believed we could fend off our demons together, but now I realized even if I did love Chad, I could not stay with him for the rest of my life. That night I promised myself that some-day I'd find a way out. But for the time being, until I had the means to support Molly and myself, I was stuck with him, the same way I'd been stuck with Mama.

"I promise baby, never again," he said.

What Chad had done was not right, but I'd been no

angel. Pushing him out the door of the trailer face first in front of his best friend was the ultimate violation of his pride. In a split second I had become my mother and I'd brought out Chad's dad in him. *Is this how our future is going to be?* I wondered. *Poor Molly. Poor baby girl.*

THE MAGIC OF FAMILY

CHAD STRAIGHTENED UP, got a handle on his drinking and stopped partying at the trailer, and I kept a watchful eye on my tendency toward violence. But things weren't the same between us. Chad's threat to shoot Molly and me had gotten stuck in the crevices of my mind.

It was becoming increasingly clear that Chad did not want me to go anywhere without him. He even insisted we get groceries together. "Anything you need Mom will have," he'd say, as he left for work. "No since getting Molly out if you don't have to."

There were things I needed that I couldn't get from Bobbi, things I didn't want to buy at the grocery store with Chad, like tampons and make-up. So sometimes I put Molly in her car seat and we went to the drug store.

Every time I went somewhere without him we had a fight. "I give you everything you need," he'd say. "All you have to do is ask. There's no reason for you to be running up and down the road burning gas we can't afford."

As long as I stayed home, everything was fine between us, so to keep peace, I stayed home. We didn't have a phone, so if I needed to call someone I had to walk down to his parents' house. Big Chad didn't like for me to make long distance calls on their phone. He had let me call Aunt Macy twice—when Chad and I got married, and when I found out I was pregnant—but Chad had to pay for the calls. The only way I could keep in touch with Aunt Macy was to give her Chad's parents' number and wait for her to call me. While Chad was at work, if I wanted to have any adult contact it would have to be with Bobbi. But we spent enough time at her house as it was, so Molly and I stayed in the trailer and entertained each other. We became best friends.

When Molly was six months old, I was changing her diaper and noticed a tiny blister-like bump about an inch from her belly button. She'd had her six month check-up days earlier and the doctor had said she was healthy, so I wasn't too concerned. I showed the blister to Chad when he got home and he thought it looked like a pimple and nothing to worry about. I doctored the bump with some Neosporin and forgot about it.

The next day, while I was giving Molly a bath, I found two more similar bumps on her torso. Now I was worried. I dressed her, put her in her carrier, and took her down to Bobbi's house. Since Bobbi had raised six kids, I was sure she would know what was wrong with Molly.

Bobby examined the blisters. "Looks to me like you've been burning her with a cigarette," she said.

"I can't believe you said that! What kind of person says something like that?"

"Well you stay held up in that trailer like a hermit. Nobody ever sees you. We don't know what you're up to in there."

"What do you mean you don't ever see me? We eat here three or four times a week. That's not enough for you?"

"When Chad's home. Who knows what goes on when he's not."

"What are you trying to say, Bobbi?"

"You're the one who said your mama abused you. Maybe you're doing what was done to you. That's what I hear happens. Abused people grow up to abuse their kids."

"I thought you didn't believe in all that *abuse* horseshit!"

"Looking at these blisters on this child I don't know what to believe!"

I picked up Molly in her carrier and started for the door. As hard as I tried not to, I broke down and started crying before I got there.

"That's right, go crawl back in your hole and hide!" Bobbi yelled, as I walked away.

"You're just mad because I don't stay right under you all the time like your kids do," I yelled back at her, sobbing. "I'm not letting you run my life like you run theirs!"

Back at the trailer, I put Molly down for a nap and had a long cry. I'd tried so hard to be a good mother, read all the books and done exactly as they said. But I now realized none of it made any difference. No matter what I did, because I'd been an abused child, as a mother I would always be examined under the bright light of suspicion.

When I stopped feeling sorry for myself, I got out all the books I'd bought on baby care and searched through every page until I found a description and pictures of bumps similar to Molly's. According to the book, she had something called impetigo, a rash caused from bacteria on the skin that could be treated with cream and antibiotics.

As soon as Molly woke up, I swallowed my pride, went back down to Bobbi's and asked her if I could use her phone to call the pediatrician to make an appointment. After I'd made the call, without saying another word, I walked back up to the trailer.

When Chad got home later that night, I told him what happened. "Aw, Mom didn't mean it," he said, like it was nothing. "She was just kidding."

"Kidding? You don't kid about stuff like that! What's wrong with *you people*?"

"Mom hasn't ever been one for thinking before she talks. She's had time to mull over it now and I'm sure she's sorry."

"So, you're taking her side?"

"Are you *asking me* to take sides?"

"Yes!"

"You want me to turn against my own mother? Just because you turned against yours doesn't mean everybody else should!"

"It always comes back to that doesn't it? I wish I'd

never told you about my abuse! You and your family are only going to use it against me!"

"You're being paranoid!" Chad said. "Nobody's using anything against you. I'm just trying to find a way to keep peace between you and Mom!"

"Good luck with that one!"

Identifying with how Chad felt about his mother was difficult, because the love I'd once had for mine had disappeared. He loved Bobbi like most people love their mothers, and that wasn't going to change. She would always be a part of his life, and as long as I was with him, she would be a part of mine.

That night, back to back, Chad and I clung to opposite edges of the bed. I wanted him to see that Bobbi had hurt me and to hold me until the pain went away, but just as I couldn't understand his feelings, he, too, was oblivious to mine. Chad was not a mean man. He was not a dumb man either. He was a man who fixed things, and if he ran across something he couldn't fix, he pushed it aside. He couldn't fix this.

We took Molly to the doctor, who examined her and said the blisters were indeed impetigo, something common in babies. He said she'd most likely picked it up from his office when we brought her in for her six week check-up, because he'd recently treated several infected kids. He gave her some antibiotics and a topical cream that made the blisters go away in a matter of days. Molly recovered without scars, but I didn't. I kept thinking about what Bobbi had said, and couldn't help but wonder if the incident was but a foreshadowing of a lifetime of being stigmatized by my abuse.

Bobbi never offered to apologize for what she said to me, even after she found out Molly's blisters were caused by impetigo. For months, I refused to go to her house to eat. Chad took Molly and went without me.

Big Chad threw a drunk about once every two or three weeks. Sometimes Trudy came to the trailer in the middle of the night to get Chad when things got bad. I didn't see the point of him getting involved, but he always went despite my protest.

Big Chad never bothered me when he threw a drunk, except once. Chad was at work on day shift, and I'd put Molly down for her afternoon nap. I decided to take advantage of the free time and relax in front of the TV. As I was about to sit on the sofa, I heard a knock on the trailer door. When I opened the door, there was Big Chad with a gun pointed at me. I tried to slam the door in his face, but he stopped me by wedging the gun between the door and the frame. He pushed himself inside the trailer and stood beside me holding the gun to the side of my head.

Maybe I should've been, but I wasn't afraid of Big Chad. I knew psycho, up close and personal, and I couldn't see it in his eyes. Maybe I was crazier than he was, because sometimes it took everything I had to keep from laughing in his face. The whole situation seemed comical to me, a wee Barney Fife of a man waving his gun around, trying to scare people, when in reality he was the one who was terrified.

"What are you doing on my goddamn property?" he asked, with a heavy tongue.

"I live here, Big Chad. You're in my trailer."

"This is *my* property!" he shouted. "And it's my damn trailer too, if I want it!"

I was afraid he would wake Molly, so I decided to try to play along with him. "You're right, Big Chad; it's your trailer. So what is it you want anyway?"

"I want you off my property!"

Not for a second did I think he had any intention of shooting me, or anyone else, on purpose, but the thought did occur to my sensible side that the gun could accidentally go off, especially with a drunk finger behind the trigger.

"Believe me, nobody wants to get off your property more than me," I assured him. "But we have to convince Chad to leave."

"Where's he at? I'll convince him!" He held the gun high in the air for emphasis.

"He's still at work, but he'll be home in about an hour and a half."

"I'll wait for him," he said, putting the gun back to my head.

"Why don't you sit on the sofa and wait?" I suggested. "I'll sit beside you so you can keep the gun to my head."

My offer seemed to confuse him. "What?"

"Why don't we sit down?"

"Sit at the table," he ordered, proving he was back in control.

I sat and so did he, laying the gun on the table in front of him. "You know I can get to this real quick if I have to," he said, patting the handle of the gun.

"Oh yeah, I know. I've seen you do it before."

He grabbed his Camels from the front pocket of his shirt and lit up.

I slid an ashtray over to him. "Want a beer?"

He looked confused again. He wasn't used to people helping him get drunker. "I'll get one if I want it." After several cheek-caving drags from his cigarette, he asked, "Who gave you permission to live here on my property anyway?"

"Chad gave me permission, but I'm not sure who gave him permission."

"Well I can tell you it wasn't me."

"I'm really sorry, Big Chad. We'll have to do something about that. Like I said, Chad will be home soon and we'll get everything straightened out then."

"Big Chad got up, waddled over to the refrigerator and pulled out a Pabst Blue Ribbon like he knew exactly where it was."

"Grab me one too, would you?" He cut his eyes over to me and studied my face for a minute, and then got another beer from the refrigerator and sat it on the table.

We sipped our beers and he smoked a few more cigarettes while another half-hour passed. He had to go to the bathroom. He picked up his gun and took it with him.

When he came out of the bathroom, I asked, "Why

don't we play cards until Chad gets home?" He loved to play cards and I knew he couldn't pass up the opportunity.

We played Black Jack for an hour and he won every hand. I made sure of it. Finally Chad walked in. He looked stunned at the sight of me and his dad sitting at the table drinking and playing cards. "Dad, what are you doing here?" he asked.

Big Chad hesitated, as if he had forgotten why he'd come. I jumped in and helped him out. "Big Chad came to ask you who gave us permission to live here."

"*You* did, Dad. You gave me permission. Don't you remember?"

"Hell no, I don't remember! I'd know if I let a chink live on my property."

We're back to the chink thing again. Funny how he never thought I was a chink. Guess it was because I was blond.

Big Chad picked up his gun from the table and aimed it at Chad. "I want you to move out today! I've got to go somewhere right now, but when I get back you both better be gone!" He chugged the rest of his beer and headed out the front door.

After Big Chad had left, Chad asked, "What was that all about?"

"What do you mean, what's it about? Your dad's on a drunk and talking nonsense again. What's new?"

For me, Big Chad getting drunk and coming up to the trailer was a good thing, because I knew I could use the incident to try to get Chad to move. I was fed up with Bobbi watching everything I did, and Chad spending all his time at their house. He'd promised me that living behind his parents was only temporary—a year at best. Over a year and a half had passed and he hadn't even mentioned moving.

"Chad, he held a gun to my head!" I said, trying to infuse fear into my voice. "What if Molly had been awake? Do you want to risk her getting shot? Do you want her to see her Papaw that way? We've got to get away from here!"

"You're right," he agreed. "We'll start looking for another place to live this weekend."

A PRETEND KIND OF HAPPY

CHAD AND I were having trouble finding a house priced within our budget. He wanted to give up the hunt, buy some land in the country and live in the trailer until we could afford to build. But he couldn't find a spot to suit him—meaning he couldn't find anything near his mom and dad. I breathed a sigh of relief when he couldn't find any land. Not only did I want to get away from Big Chad and Bobbi, I wanted to get away from the trailer too. I hated its thin paneled walls and foam ceilings, how every time a big storm came I could hear it popping and creaking, and feel it swaying in the wind.

It took a few months, but Chad finally did sell the trailer to his friend, Harry, and we bought a tiny frame house in a subdivision on the outskirt of Sullivan. As soon as I saw the house, I knew it was going to be ours. I pictured Chad grilling burgers out in the yard while Molly played with the neighborhood kids. Of course Molly would have to make some friends, and we would have to buy a grill, but those were minor details.

The new house had only a tad more room inside than the trailer, but the place was sturdy, in decent shape and within our budget. Chad hated the idea of living in a subdivision. "Everybody's on top of each other here," he complained. "You can reach out the window and shake hands with your neighbors while they're sitting in their living room." He promised that as soon as some land he liked became available we were going to start building. I prayed that would never happen.

The house was tight, but at least it had a concrete foundation and a real roof. And there was a neighborhood, a neighborhood with a quiet street on which I could take walks and push Molly in her stroller. But the best part was there would be no meddling, controlling Bobbi around, or little Big Chad wielding his gun.

After a while, Chad came around and began sharing my enthusiasm for the new house. Together we painted the living room and kitchen walls a cheerful sunshine yellow to match the gold carpet and white linoleum floors. Each of the three bedrooms had a different color of shag carpet: hunter green, Royal blue, and deep crimson. We bought wallpaper on clearance to coordinate with each bedroom: trees for the green one, cloudy skies for the blue, and for our room, we chose a red and cream velvet fleur de lei pattern. By the time we'd hung red sheers on the windows, put up our yard sale brass bed, and decorated with peacock feathers and a lava lamp, our bedroom looked like a brothel. At the time, I thought it was stunning, especially in the early morning when the sun shone through the sheers bathing my skin in a flattering pink light.

Molly, now nine months old, was crawling and pulling up, and getting into everything. She could say *Mama, Daddy, birdie, no, baba* for bottle, and, *ta-ta,* which was what she called her security blanket. She was such a good baby, and a daddy's girl. Her face lit up every time she had him in her sight. And she was so beautiful. She looked like a china doll with her dark, almost black hair, rosy cheeks, and deep hazel eyes. All—well most—parents think their children are beautiful, but ours really was. We had people stop us on the streets to tell us so.

One of my younger brothers, Jimmy D. had recently graduated from high school and had moved into an apartment in Uniontown, a few miles away from where Chad and I lived. He'd always liked the area when we were kids and had made many friends there during his teenage years. Shortly after he moved there, he looked us up and started visiting the house, and slowly, we got to know each other again and established an on the surface friendship.

Whenever I tried to bring up our past, Jimmy D., like Mama, didn't want to discuss it. He was careful not to mention her during our conversations. The few times her name did slip through his lips, his face went pale, like a snake had been released into the room. I knew better than to say anything bad about her to him, or to suggest he should condemn her for what she'd done to me. How could I expect him to turn against her when she'd been so good to him?

Once, late at night, after a few beers, I cajoled him in to talking. He acknowledged, in a general way, that Mama didn't treat me the same as her other children, but the minute I tried to expand on the subject, he became defensive as if he thought I was blaming him for not doing something to save me. I wasn't. If I couldn't help myself, how could I have expected him to help me?

As we were talking, I was taken back to a time when he was eight and I was around ten. Mama had created a contest between him and my other two brothers to see which one of them could hit me in the stomach the hardest. To appease her, he had cocked his arm and pretended he was going to hit me hard, but then right as the punch met my stomach, he held back. I had never forgotten his brave act of kindness, only a child himself.

I wondered if in the ten years since, he'd ever thought of that day, or any of our shared incidents of abuse. I wondered if, looking back through the eyes of an adult, his perception was skewed. If he found it difficult to recreate how he felt then—the terror, the sense of helplessness—because to acknowledge the feelings he'd had as a boy, might make him seem weak as a man.

The last thing I wanted from Jimmy D. was guilt, or an apology, or for us to relive the details of the depressing history we'd shared. I only wanted him to admit the atrocities I endured—the atrocities we both endured. You begin to think you're crazy when everyone around you pretends something never happened when you know damn well it did. Makes you think you're viewing life through a dirty window. You question yourself—your memory, your sanity. *Did it actually happen?*

There were many things I wanted to say to Jimmy D., but whenever he displayed reticence, I retreated out of fear of running him off, of losing him altogether. Because I wanted to keep him—the only semblance of a sibling I had—in my life, I chose to move forward with our relationship as if our past did not exist. What I had with Jimmy D. wasn't much, but it was *something,* something that made me feel closer to normal. More than what I had before he moved back to Kentucky. Before he came along, things had been lopsided with Chad's huge extended family—albeit dysfunctional—to share with Molly, and no one but Aunt Macy to represent my side. Molly loved Jimmy D.'s funny, lighthearted ways, and he was good with her. He and Chad got along too. They had a few guy's nights out, drinking beer and shooting pool.

Things were better than they'd ever been for me. I had a husband, a daughter, a house, and now I had a brother. Chad had cut back on his drinking, and the only time he partied was when he occasionally went out to a bar with his sisters or Jimmy D. He never wanted me to go to the bars with them; I was the one left at home to babysit all the kids. On the outside, I wore a serene smile, but below the surface, I harbored a troubling secret: trapped under Chad's protective net disguised as love, I had become a prisoner, like I'd been as a child and I dreamt of the day I would break free.

On a gorgeous morning in early summer, I decided to take Molly down to the local Kwik Pik for a Popsicle. I dressed her in her cutest sun-suit and strapped her in her car seat. As I started the car engine, I noticed I felt awkward behind the wheel, almost as if I were driving for the very first time. Figuring it was because I hadn't been out in a while, I ignored the strange feeling and shifted into reverse.

Backing out of the driveway, my pulse quickened and my chest began to get tight. I put the car in park again to collect myself. For a minute or two, I sat there in a cold sweat, not sure what to do next. *Maybe I'm coming down with something,* I thought. I decided to skip the Popsicles and go back into the house.

I shut off the engine and turned to unstrap Molly from her car seat. She smiled at me with all four teeth visible, excited to be going somewhere. When I started to get her out, she began to whimper. I'd already told her we were going to get a Popsicle and she was looking forward to it. I didn't have the heart to let her down. I squared up with the steering wheel again. *How difficult can this be?* The Kwik Pik was less than five miles away. *I can do this.* I backed the rest of the way out of the driveway, both clammy hands glued to the wheel at ten and two.

Once we got going, the other cars appeared to me as if they were driving too close to mine, causing me to swerve off the road. All at once, everything around me— buildings and houses I'd seen hundreds of times before— looked unfamiliar. There was no way I could have been lost. I knew the Kwik Pik was a short, straight shot on the highway from our house, but it seemed like I'd been driving forever. *Did I turn the wrong way coming out of the subdivision?*

Resisting the urge to turn the car around, I drove a little farther down the road, until I spotted the familiar red and white Kwik Pik sign. I'd never in my life been so glad to see a convenient store. Carrying Molly on one hip, I went inside and browsed around. When I had been in there so long the clerk began to eye me suspiciously, I paid for our Popsicles and took them out to the car to eat.

After we finished, we sat in the parking lot for almost an hour watching the traffic go by. I was stalling because I was afraid to drive back home. Molly was hot and was beginning to get fussy. She was sticky from the Popsicle and her diaper needed to be changed. Chad would be off work soon. We had to go home.

Clenching the steering wheel in a death grip, I started the car and pulled out, my heart drumming in my ears. When we got home, I grabbed Molly and ran inside the house. I wasn't sure what had just happened, but I decided not to tell anyone.

A day or two later, Chad went squirrel hunting on some rural land out by his parents' house. I refused to eat squirrel meat, but Bobbi liked it, so he always dropped off whatever he shot with her.

As soon as he walked in the door from hunting, he asked me what I was doing at the Kwik Pik a few days earlier.

"How did you know I was at the Kwik Pik?"

"Mom told me. She said somebody she knew saw you there sitting in the parking lot."

"I can't believe this town is so frickin' small that I can't even go to the Kwik Pik without Bobbi knowing about it."

"What I want to know is why you didn't tell *me* you went!"

"*Tell you* I went to get a Popsicle for Molly? I didn't *tell you* because I didn't think it was important!"

"We're married; we're supposed to tell each other everything!"

"It's the Kwik Pik for heaven sake!" I was waving my hands and my voice was squeaky. I sounded guilty. "Why did Bobbi tell you I was there, anyway? And why did whoever told her think to mention it?" I leaned in. "What, do you have people watching me now?"

"Something like that."

"Oh my god! I'm surrounded by nuts! And your mom and her friends are a bunch of no-life hicks!"

"You're awfully defensive for somebody who just went out to get a Popsicle!"

"This is ridiculous!" I went into the kitchen to finish making dinner.

He followed me. "I'll tell you what's ridiculous. My wife sitting in the Kwik Pik parking lot for hours like some whore trying to pick up a john!"

Chad started drinking, and we stayed up all night saying the same things over and over, getting nowhere. It was exhausting.

He and I had begun to argue a lot lately. We didn't

fight physically like we had when we first got together—having a child in the house had changed that—but our shouting matches were over the top, and often caused Molly to cry. All the screaming and threats took me back to a place where I didn't want to be. And when Chad pushed me too far, my own pent up rage sometimes gurgled to the surface. To keep the wild animal inside of me tame, I got to where I would do almost anything to avoid a fight, which meant letting Chad have his way.

After the Kwik Pik issue, I stayed home and played the good wife, the good mother. Going to the convenient store wasn't worth fighting over. I was too scared to drive anyway. I even broke over and started going with Chad to his parents' house again. Not much had changed there during my brief boycott: Big Chad ignored me as usual, and his sisters tolerated me because they had to. But for some reason—probably guilt—Bobbi was nice to me. She even offered to give me a home perm, for which she claimed to be famous. I was leery of the idea, but felt obligated to accept her peace offering.

Bobbi got out a shoe box of well-used pink curlers and rolled my hair so tightly my eyebrows took on a sinister upward slant. When she'd finished with me, my hair was frizzy and had turned from dirty blond to a pale orangey color. But it didn't matter; I wasn't planning on getting out of the house much anyway.

Chad had me where he wanted me: at home with a child, my only adult contact being him and his family. Still I was convinced he loved me, and that his controlling behavior was born of his determination to hold together the family he'd created. I wasn't sure exactly what, from his dysfunctional upbringing, had caused him to have such deep-seeded insecurities. He was no doubt, like me, concealing ghosts from his past even more disturbing than the ones I'd already seen. Chad and I had both been damaged by our disturbed parents, and the damage had perpetuated our own familial dysfunction. Even if we could somehow repair what our parents had done to us, it would surely not be a quick fix—or an easy one.

POSSIBILITIES

MOLLY AND I were out in the backyard one afternoon when I heard a sunny female voice coming from around the side of the house. "Hello?"

Turning in the direction of the voice, I saw a young woman leaning over the top of the chain-link fence, holding a baby boy who appeared to be around Molly's age. I recognized the woman as one of the neighbors who lived across the street. Once while walking, I'd passed her house when she was out in her yard watering flowers, and she had smiled and waved at me in a friendly, neighborly way.

"Hi," I said to her.

She smiled. "Mind if we come around back?"

"No, not at all; the gate's unlocked."

As they approached us, recalling how pretty this woman was, I regretted not having put on make-up, and also for agreeing to let Bobbi give me a home perm.

"Hi, I'm Mindy Olson, and this is my son, Joey." She

turned and pointed to a brick house across the street, diagonal to ours. "We live over there."

"Yeah, I know, I sometimes see you when I'm out walking. My name is Tuesday, and this is Molly."

"Did you say Tuesday? Like... *today*?"

I laughed. "Yes, I know it's unusual. My mother named me after the movie star, Tuesday Weld. She had a thing about naming all her kids after famous people."

"Hmmm, I don't think I've ever heard of Tuesday Weld. Pretty name, though. I like Molly, too. Did you name her after Molly Ringwald?"

The possibility that I was subconsciously trying to imitate Mama by naming Molly after a movie star had never entered my mind. The thought of it disturbed me. "No, I didn't," I said.

I unfolded another lawn chair for Mindy and we sat and talked while the kids played together. We instantly clicked, like the snap on my favorite jeans. Mindy told me she had another child, a daughter, named Charity, who was in the first grade. She mentioned her sister and mother several times, which indicated she was close to her family and saw them on a regular basis. Twice, during our conversation, I went out of my way to bring up Jimmy D. to show her I had a family too, and didn't just crawl out from under a rock somewhere. "You may have heard of my *brother*, Jimmy D. Storm," I said. "He was an athlete in high school and really popular." And then later, I mentioned that I needed to think of something good to have for supper. "My *brother*, Jimmy D., may be coming over."

Mindy was everything I wasn't but had always wanted to be: pretty, confident and athletic, which meant she'd also been popular in high school, something else I never was. It didn't take long for me to become smitten with her. The possibilities of where our friendship could go were exciting. She played on a volleyball team, which she invited me to join. She told me she and Chad had gone to high school together, although she didn't have much to say about him. My guess was they didn't run in the same circles. I also found out one of her best friends was someone I'd known for a short period of time when I was in junior high school.

"So you know Katrina?" Mindy asked. "Wait until I tell her you're my neighbor!"

"She probably won't remember me," I said. My impact on Katrina's life was probably insignificant, but I'd never forgotten her because she had done something that touched my then miserable life in a special way.

It was my last year at home, on Thanksgiving Day. I was outside raking the front yard, when through the swooshing of the leaves came a clip-clop, clip-clop, clip-clop, like the hooves of a horse clunking the road. I turned to see a thin, shaggy-haired girl around my age perched high on a pair of wooden clogs. She stopped in front of the yard and flashed a toothy smile. "Ello!" she said. "I'm Katrina, and I just moved here from England. I live a few blocks up the road. What is your name?"

"Tuesday," I said.

"Is your last name Storm?" she asked.

"Yes."

"I believe my father works with yours at the Job Corps Center. He was transferred here from London," she said. "Why are you raking leaves on Thanksgiving, Tuesday?"

"Just doing what I was told."

"Well I'll have none of that! Not on Thanksgiving!" Then she clip-clopped up the sidewalk to my house and knocked on the front door. Watching her, I was puzzled, wondering what on earth she was doing.

Mama opened the door. "Ello, Mrs. Storm," Katrina said. "Sorry to be a bother on Thanksgiving. I'm Katrina Baker, and my father works with your husband. I wanted to let you know that Tuesday is coming with me to my house for a while." Then she fluttered her fingers at Mama as she started back down the porch steps. "Cheers!" she said, and then clip-clopped down the sidewalk to me. "Come along, Tuesday."

I spent the rest of the day at Katrina house, stuffing myself on a massive spread of Thanksgiving food. There were cold cuts, and cheese trays lined with fancy crackers, and shrimp with cocktail sauce, and a heavenly fruit and cake dessert Katrina's mom called trifle. Katrina's spunkiness fascinated me, and I could've spent hours listening to her talk, even though I often had trouble understanding what she was saying through her heavy British accent.

When I got home that night, Mama was infuriated, and of course, I suffered the consequences, but spending the day with Katrina was worth it. Later, I found out Katrina's father was ranked above mine at the Job Corps Center where they worked, so when she had introduced herself as the boss's daughter, Mama couldn't risk one of daddy's superiors becoming suspicious and discovering what occurred behind the closed doors of our house. She had no choice but to let me go with Katrina. I found this to be amusing, and wondered if Katrina knew this and had cleverly used it to her advantage.

Katrina questioned why, whenever she came by my house, I was always working, and why I never got to go anywhere outside of school like other kids. Although, because of my shame, I never came right out and explained to her the gory details of how I was treated, I could tell she sensed something was not right about my life at home. From time to time, she would knock on my door and rescue me for a while, and I loved her for that. When I moved away to Nashville to live with Aunt Macy, we lost touch, but I'd thought about her often and wondered what became of her.

When Chad got home from work, I was hesitant to tell him I'd made a new friend. In the past, he had been jealous when I gave my attention to anyone other than him. But when I told him about Mindy he didn't seem too bothered. At the time, he had no idea how close we would become.

Before Mindy came along, taking care of Molly, playing with her, had been what I lived for. While Chad was at work, when I wasn't playing dolls with her in her room, I hovered over her while she splashed in her kiddie pool in the backyard. As her only playmate, I was able to be the child I never got to be, but I sometimes wondered if she needed the company of other kids her age. Molly was still the center of my life, but now that I had another adult to talk to while Chad was at work, I didn't smother her so much.

Both Chad and Mindy's husband, Jack, had day shift jobs at local coal mines. While they were at work, either I was at Mindy's house, or she was at mine. We spent the mornings outside working on our tans, while Molly and Joey played in the kiddie pool. Molly looked forward to her playtime with Joey, and it was good for her to have a friend her age.

If we wanted to go shopping, or take the kids for ice-cream, Mindy always drove us. She didn't mind; she was a skilled, confident driver. I had not been able to bring myself to drive a car since my panic attack on my way to the Kwik Pik. I'd tried a few times, but the minute I got behind the wheel my heart raced and I sometimes became dizzy and nauseous. I didn't understand, or know how to deal with my sudden phobia that had erupted from out of nowhere, so I simply pushed it from my mind.

In the afternoons, around two-thirty or three o'clock, Mindy and I parted ways to do our housework and cook for our families. My friendship with her didn't interfere with my marriage as long as I kept the house clean and had supper on the table before Chad got home. But there were days when his mine would strike for some silly reason, like the bath house being dirty, and in less than an hour after he left for work he would come right back. When this happened, he called Mindy's house and insisted Molly and I return home. One day the time got away from Mindy and me, and she was still at the house when Chad came in. Chad embarrassed me by being rude to her then, reminding me how jealous and possessive he could be.

REFLECTIONS OF A GIRL
CALLED HORSE FACE

WHILE I WAS pregnant, Chad and I may have wanted Molly to be a boy, but the instant we saw her we fell hopelessly in love with our adorable baby girl. By the time she was walking, she had blossomed into a truly stunning child. Even though I was uncertain of my own self-image, I was confident in Molly's overt beauty. But it wasn't enough that I knew she was beautiful; I wanted to make everyone else aware too. And I wanted her to learn the power of her beauty, and relish the self-esteem it would bring—self-esteem of which I'd been robbed.

When Molly was three-years-old, I entered her in the Little Miss contest at the local fair. She didn't win, but she came in the top five. Naturally, I was disappointed because I thought she should have at least placed in the top three. When the Uniontown Trade Days fall festival rolled around in August, I signed her up for their Little

Miss contest, and she got third runner up. Again I thought she should have done better, but I was still thrilled—a bit too thrilled.

All the attention and compliments Molly received from placing in the Little Miss Trade Days contest gave me a rush of pride unlike anything I'd experienced before. I didn't want the high to end. I thought if I could enter her in one more contest, she would surely win. Mindy told me about more local beauty pageants her daughter, Charity had been in, and said if I wanted to enter Molly in some of them, she would be glad to help. Without hesitation, I dove in head first.

The first thing I found out when I entered the pageant scene was there was always an entry fee, and sometimes it was significant. The designer dresses the girls wore were expensive too, running anywhere from 85 to 100 dollars. Since we now had a house payment, and were still paying on Chad's expensive sport car, we couldn't afford a suitable pageant dress for Molly to wear in her competitions, so I decided to buy the material and sew a dress for her myself.

The more I got into the pageants, the more I realized how difficult and competitive they were. Molly had to learn to walk a certain way, stand a certain way. Keeping up with the other contestants took a lot of hard work on her part. While the neighborhood kids were playing outdoors, she was rehearsing her poses, practicing her fake smile.

Copying from the other girls—that undoubtedly had professional coaches—I created a stage routine for Molly.

We were both in her bedroom one day, going over the routine, when I noticed she seemed disinterested in learning what I was trying to teach her. After hours of practicing the same poses again and again, she still wasn't catching on. My impatience was starting to simmer. "Your feet have to be angled when you stop in front of the judges!" I said, frustration dripping from my words. She directed her eyes to the floor in shame. I reached over and lifted her chin. "And you can't look down—ever. You have to keep your head up and smile at the judges! Now try again, and this time *concentrate!*"

In Molly's vanity mirror, I caught a glimpse of Mama's enraged face. Her teeth were gritted and the veins in her neck were bulging. I looked at Molly and it struck me how sad and frightened she appeared, and how tiny and helpless she was compared to me towering over her. I bolted from the room, and Molly chased after me. "What's wrong Mama?" she called out. "Come back, please! I'll try harder!"

Trembling, I sat at the kitchen table and buried my face in my hands. "No honey, you've practiced enough for the day," I said, trying to hide the concern in my voice. "You go outside now and play a while."

After she left the kitchen I crumbled. *What the hell is wrong with me? Am I becoming my mother?* I'd heard Chad's sisters scream at their kids dozens of times and had never thought they were being abusive. Even Mindy, always a calm and understanding parent, sometimes had to raise her voice to get Joey's attention. Why, when I did the same thing, did it seem much worse? The reality—my reality—was because of what happened to me as a child, I didn't have the luxury of behaving like other mothers, because my actions would always be scrutinized, if not by others, then by me.

After searching my mind for solutions and finding none, I did what all the Storms before me had done when faced with a situation they didn't know how to handle—I pushed the incident from my mind and pretended it had never happened. *It will never happen again,* I promised myself.

But it did happen again. And again. The possibility of becoming my mother scared me so much I began to refrain from doing anything in the way of discipline for fear I would make the wrong move. Instead I put the burden on Chad, making him the bad guy. Thankfully Molly was a good child and it didn't take much to keep her in line.

After several months of pageant after pageant, I began to notice how sometimes after a competition Molly seemed downhearted. There were even times when she broke into tears, particularly if she didn't place. I told myself she was crying because she didn't win. But she wasn't. She was only three years old; she didn't care about winning. She was crying because she sensed how important it was to *me* that she win, and when she didn't she thought she'd let me down. The pageants were filling a need inside of me, but they were doing nothing at all for Molly, except making her feel inadequate. Plus they were costing our family money we didn't have to spend.

I'd done this to my daughter. *I* had done this to her.

I'd been telling everyone Molly wanted to compete, but that wasn't true. The pageants weren't about her. They were about me and my obsession with beauty, the beauty Mama had never allowed me to have. Molly's beauty had become my beauty, the pageants had become my pageants, and when she won I won. I was doing to her the same injustice Mama had done to me, only at the other extreme. Where Mama had once been obsessed with what she perceived as my ugliness, I had become obsessed with Molly's beauty. And like Mama, I was sending the wrong message to my daughter by putting too much emphasis on the importance of appearance, embedding in her psyche what had been embedded in mine— the beautiful are superior and powerful, and the ugly are weak and worthless.

Seeing her in pain—unnecessary pain I had caused— made me relive the sense of inadequacy I had experienced when I first realized I was a failure in my own mother's eyes. It tore at my heart to think Molly was now experiencing what I had felt then. Although I didn't want to, I put a stop to the pageants. Her last competition was the Little Miss contest at the fair when she was four, which she won. Mindy's son, Joey won for the boys. The two of them being crowned Little Mr. and Miss Uniontown Fair was as gratifying an ending to the pageants as I was ever going to get.

After I stopped entering Molly in pageants, I was immediately aware of the void. My preoccupation with her beauty had temporarily sidetracked me from focusing on my physical flaws, flaws Mama had pointed out almost every day of my childhood. When I was busy preparing for a competition, my angular jawline, stringy blond hair and thick lips didn't seem to matter so much. It was easier to hide, with some heavy bangs and artful application of makeup, the girl my mother had once called Horse Face.

Now that I had more free time on my hands, my insecurities compelled me to begin obsessing about my appearance. I kept a compact mirror with me, which I checked compulsively, because I always had the nagging notion that my mascara was melting, or my lipstick was smudged or, the concealer had worn off a zit I was trying to hide. But my fussiness about my appearance was all in vain, because regardless of how much make-up I piled on, I could see Horse Face peering at me from underneath. She was still alive and I'd yet to silence my mother's words that continued to echo from the past.

Chad was not the type of man to tell me what I needed to hear to boost my self-esteem. In his way of thinking, I should already know he thought I was attractive because he married me. Mindy doled out the typical woman to woman compliments about my clothes and hair, but I knew women did that to be nice. She was a great friend, but sometimes being around her only fed my insecurities. She was the kind of woman Mama, with her irrational jealousy of all attractive women, would have secretly hated. Mama preferred light hair over dark, and soft, feminine facial features were a must, instead of the angular jawline of Horse Face. She also thought it was important for a woman to be petite. Tall and gangly like me was

a sure kiss of death. Athletic was good—muscular cheerleader types—like Mama had been when she was high
school. Mindy was all that with a sultry voice to boot.

It was no surprise Mindy had a way with men, and
her skills in this area came in handy when I was trying to persuade Chad to let me play on her volleyball
team. We caught him at a good time because I'd recently
approached him about getting a job, and he preferred me
playing volleyball one night a week to possibly being
gone every day.

I was pumped about playing volleyball. Sports were in
my DNA, and a part of my history. Daddy had played
basketball in high school and college. Then he became an
athletic coach, and refereed football and basketball games
on the side. Growing up, my brothers had participated
in every sport possible, and my parents had oohed and
aahed over their accomplishments. But I was uncoordi-
nated and clumsy, and I had never played a sport in my
life.

"I've never played volleyball," I warned Mindy for
the umpteenth time as we pulled into the parking lot of
the gym where we were playing our first game of the
season.

"Don't worry about it," she said. "We play for fun
anyway."

"Good, because I don't want to mess up your team."

"You won't," Mindy assured me. "By the way, Katrina
is excited to see you again."

I'm sure you had to remind her who I was. "Really, she is? She remembers me?"

"Yes! She said you were one of her best friends in school."

Mindy opened the gym door and we both entered. Inside was bright and noisy, and the air was moist and salty with the smell of sweat. When Katrina spotted me, she came up and gave me a hug that seemed genuine. *She does remember me.*

"Tuesday! How are you?" Her British accent was not as prominent as it once had been because she'd lived in Kentucky for so long. She looked almost the same as she had when we were in school together: shaggy brown hair and a contagious, toothy smile. She was even as tiny as she had been years ago.

"I'm good, much better than I was when you knew me before."

"Yeah, your parents were mean to you weren't they?"

"My mother."

She didn't know the details, and I had no intention of telling her, or Mindy. I didn't want to ruin the sense of normalcy I'd begun to feel. I quickly changed the subject. "I'm married now and I have daughter."

"Me too, but I have a son," she said. "I wouldn't have recognized you if you weren't with Mindy!" she squealed. "You've changed so much!" She was right; I had changed. I'd been working hard on my appearance lately. I had grown my hair out to a perfect Farrah Fawcett style, and I wore a lot more make-up.

Mindy introduced me to the rest of the team. They

were all pretty and warm like her. Surrounded by them, for a few minutes, I almost felt like I was living out the high school experience I'd always fantasized about. Like I was part of a group, a clique, one of the *popular* girls.

Everything was perfect until the game began, and my fantasy turned into a nightmare. Every time the ball came to me, I either missed it altogether, or hit it into the bleachers. The other girls on the team said it was okay, but they couldn't hide their spontaneous expressions of disappointment and frustration whenever I screwed up another play.

I sucked so bad at volleyball, Mindy and the other women on the team probably wished I would quit, but I wanted to continue playing. For the first time in my life, I was an insider instead of an outcast, and I wasn't about to give that up. But I didn't want to cause the team to lose every game either, so I had to find a way to get good fast.

Volleyball became the obsession that replaced Molly's pageants. I got Chad to buy me a ball, and I practiced by myself every day, every spare second I had. I hit the ball off the side of the house and threw it in the air and bumped it over and over again, hundreds of times. Even when the weather was cold, I still practiced with numb fingers. In a matter of weeks, I wasn't a pro, but I was as good as everybody else on the team.

It was a Monday night; Molly was in bed and Chad was enthralled in a football game. I poured myself a glass of wine and slipped off into our bedroom for some me time.

Earlier in the day, I'd watched a show on television about a disfigured girl with a skin-hardening disease called scleroderma, and I couldn't shake the thought of her from my head. Her physical and emotional suffering, and social struggles in life, had been far beyond anything I'd gone through, or could ever imagine, and yet, every time the cameras were on her, she was smiling and bubbly. Somehow this wonderful, but unfortunate child was able to gain confidence in spite of her predicament. She proved that what goes on inside your head—despite what you are on the outside—is one of the key ingredients in a happy life.

No matter what other people thought of me, what I believed was my reality, and I believed what I'd been told over and over as a child, that I was worthless and ugly and a burden to those around me. I knew I would never be truly happy from within, like the girl with scleroderma, until I found a way to build my self-esteem. "Happiness is a choice," the talk show host had said. Sounded simple; but was I strong enough to pull it off?

I slid out from under the bed, an old shoebox of mementoes I'd collected during the first few years after I left home, at around fourteen. The box—I called it my box of memories—contained photos of my family that Daddy had given me, birthday cards he'd sent, and scraps of paper on which I'd scribbled rough renderings of what I remembered from my early childhood. As I lifted the lid, I saw a photograph of Mama sitting on the front steps of our house on Maplewood Drive. The photo was on top, because it was the one I always took out when I felt the way I did that night.

The last time I'd seen Mama was at Shoney's over five years earlier, and since then, I'd lost all desire to have her in my life, and I'd let go of the hope that we could foster a meaningful mother-daughter relationship. The more I was away from her, the less I wanted to see her. Molly certainly didn't need a grandmother like Mama. She had Aunt Macy, and Jimmy D., and Chad's tightly-woven kin were always within shouting distance. And now there was Mindy, Joey and Charity, who'd become like family to Molly and me. We had love and support at every turn in our lives, so we didn't need Mama around messing things up with her crazy ways.

No I didn't want to see Mama ever again, and I didn't want her anywhere near Molly. However I still had the same unanswered questions as always rattling around in my brain. On this night, as I pulled Mama's photo from the box of memories, I had one in particular in mind: Why had she been so obsessed with the way I looked? Examining the photo, I wondered: *Did she really think I was ugly, or was it her way of justifying her rejection of me?*

Chad walked in. "Game's over," he said. He looked over my shoulder at the photo. "That your mama?"

"Yes, when she was about my age."

He took the picture from me for a closer look. "You know you favor her, don't you?"

After all she'd done to me, I should have been offended by his observation—appalled. But I wasn't. Instead, my chest swelled with pathetic pride, recalling how beautiful everyone had said she was. "You think so? Really?" I said, almost giddy. "Then why did she tell me I was ugly all my life?"

"Probably because she was jealous of you," he said, without hesitation, as if it was obvious and I was dumb for not seeing it. I'd always admired—and maybe envied—his it-is-what-it- is viewpoint. The way he was able to take life at face value and never over think a situation, like I had a tendency to do. To Chad, there were no gray areas, only his solid truth, and you either accepted it or you moved on.

"Jealous? But I was just a kid?"

"Maybe she wasn't so much jealous of *you* as she was the fact that you're a girl. You did say you were the only girl, didn't you?"

"Except for my half-sister, Audrey."

"Yeah, well she don't count because she was crippled. You can't be jealous of a cripple," he said, as if it were some sort of universally accepted rule.

"Guess not."

"That's the only thing it could be, because you're *not* ugly."

I smiled, and enjoyed the moment, knowing it was the closest thing to a compliment I would ever get from him. He handed me the picture and walked away. "I'm gonna make a run to the liquor store to get some beer. Be back in a few."

As he left the room, I considered his theory. True, it probably didn't help that I'd been born a girl. From an early age, Mama had learned that in order to get what was important to her she had to compete with the females around her. She had to beat out the other girls in her school to win head cheerleader and homecoming queen. At home, she had to vie with her mother and sister for her father's attention. Then as a woman, she had to use her beauty to find herself a husband who would be willing to take care of her and her polio-stricken child. Truth be known, she didn't want to have a daughter in the first place, because it would only create unwanted competition for the attention of the men in her life. Had Audrey not become sick with polio she could have been at risk for becoming a target for Mama's jealous rage. So, if Chad was right, in a way, being sick had saved Audrey. I pondered for a minute thinking about that. *Would I have rather had polio than to have suffered the brutal childhood I did?* I wasn't sure.

Maybe when Mama gave birth to me, another girl, once again, her territory was threatened. Her jealousy and resentment of me could have been lying dormant inside her for years, and then awakened by her fall down the basement stairs. She wanted to believe I was an ugly child, both to justify, in her mind, her rejection of me, and also because she couldn't bear the thought of another female getting more attention than her. She couldn't risk the chance of me growing up to be prettier than she was, and that wasn't beyond the realm of possibility. After all, I had her genes. So to protect her territory, she first convinced herself I was ugly, and then she convinced my father and brothers. Then when I got older and became more of a threat, to make sure all bases were covered, she manipulated my appearance to make me as unattractive as she possibly could. That's why she chopped my hair off and made me go for weeks without washing it, and sent me to school in hideous, outdated clothes.

Tipsy from the wine, as I studied the picture, I let down my guard and allowed my mind to wander back to a place I swore I'd never go again... *The school bus is pulling away. With my book satchel pressed hard against my chest, I am running to catch the bus, cutting across yards to get there quicker. My scalp is numb and my hair is heavy, like I'm wearing a thick, wet wig. With numb fingers, I grope at my soapy, partially frozen hair. As I run, I scold myself: "How could I be so stupid to think I could wash my hair outside in freezing temperature!" Against the winter wind, I pull up the collar of the ancient "clown coat" with buttons like Frisbees that Mama had given me to wear. My running is clumsy and impaired by the two-sizes-too-big men's boots I am wearing. Boarding the bus, dread engulfs me. I pass the driver, who stifles a chuckle and looks away, and then I turn to face the kids. "High Waters!" someone shouts—it's the nickname they've given me because I wear pants that hit mid-calf—"What did you do to your hair? Did you fall in the water you were wading in?" Suddenly I'm surrounded by laughing faces and bobbing heads, and I want to disappear...*

LEGACY DENIED

CHAD WANTED ANOTHER baby. He was ready to shoot for a boy, but because he and I both had come from dysfunctional families, I didn't want to push our luck. Chad didn't understand my rationale, and kept trying to persuade me to change my mind, arguing that Molly, being an only child, would one day miss a sibling relationship. He made a good point. I, having been alienated from my brothers, often wondered about the special bond between siblings I'd missed out on. Because I didn't want my daughter to experience this loneliness, I began warming up to the idea of having another child. I decided to go off the pill and see what happened.

Practically the next day after I stopped taking the pill, I became pregnant. In my conscious mind I knew it was going to happen, but still, like when I found out I was having Molly, my initial reaction was alarm. Even though I'd never felt an iota of inclination to do any of the sadistic things to Molly that Mama had done to me, and I'd learned to make a vigilant effort to monitor my discipline of her, I knew, because Mama hadn't mistreated all of her children, I had not moved past the threat of inheriting her legacy of abusive behavior. And then there was the chance I would suddenly snap like she did. I was still aware of the anger churning around inside of me—anger that had caused me to attack Mama when I was a teenager, and throw Chad and his friend out of the trailer.

In the early part of my pregnancy, I had some morning sickness, but nothing even close to what I'd experienced when I was carrying Molly. My appetite was good and I put on weight at a steady rate. When I went for a sonogram, this time the sex of the baby was obvious. We were having a boy.

This was good news for Chad, who'd always wanted a son, and for me too, because I'd gotten the idea in my head that I would be less likely to abuse a boy. Molly was glad to hear she was getting a brother, that way she could be the only girl. Regardless of whether the baby was a boy or a girl, I had already made up my mind that I didn't want any more than two children. If everything went well, Molly would have a sibling and Chad, a son. No more tempting fate. I asked my doctor to schedule me for a tubal ligation after my delivery.

For the most part, my pregnancy was uneventful. I felt good—sometimes better than when I wasn't pregnant—and I had a healthy appetite. Having always been hungry as a child, now that I could justify eating what I wanted when I wanted, I became like a starving animal. Chad said I ate like a man, even when I wasn't pregnant, and truthfully he was being kind, because I ate *more* than most men I knew. Now, eating for two, I sometimes put away as many calories as an Olympic athlete.

Because of all the work Mama had made me do when I was a kid, I'd developed a keen metabolism, and had never had to worry too much about gaining weight. If I did gain a few pounds, I was able to lose them in a few weeks. But my keen metabolism deserted me when I became pregnant the second time. Every day I woke up fatter than the day before. Chad didn't seem to mind, and Bobbi kept heaping buttery mashed potatoes and macaroni and cheese on my plate "to make sure that boy's healthy." Six months into my pregnancy, I'd gained so much weight I could no longer bend over to give myself a pedicure. Although I couldn't talk Chad in to painting my toenails, he at least agreed to clip them for me.

Because we knew the sex of the baby, we began to consider boy's names early on. Chad surprised me by saying he didn't want the baby to be named after him. By the time I was seven months along, we had decided on the name, Daryl. I liked it because I didn't know of any famous people by that name.

We knew exactly when Daryl was coming. Because my delivery of Molly had been rough, the doctor didn't want our second baby to be any bigger, so he decided when I neared my due date, he would induce labor. The magic day was April 15, and when it rolled around, I was more than ready to unload ten pounds of the sixty I'd gained.

The labor wasn't bad. The drugs were good, and the baby came out healthy and a boy like the doctor had said. Chad floated through the hospital with a big grin on his face. Molly was tickled with her new baby brother too. Bobbi and Big Chad were beaming with pride, even though Big Chad had to concede to being wrong when he'd said we'd have half a dozen "split tails" before we got a boy. "You got lucky," he said.

Daryl was cute; he resembled Molly when she was a newborn, but with less hair. Despite my fears, in the months after he was born, I had no hint of an urge to do him any harm. He and Molly were my purpose in life, my salvation. Their unconditional love had begun to repair my fractured heart, and caring for them kept my mind from slipping back into the black hole of my childhood. Once again, my days were full, my life was full, and my heart was overflowing with joy. I had two healthy children and a husband who worked hard to support us. What more could I want?

THE OTHER GRANDMOTHER

A ROUND DARYL'S FIRST birthday, Aunt Macy and Edwin stopped in for a visit on their way to see some of Edwin's relatives in Ohio. We sat in the living room, sipping lemonade, talking mostly about the kids. Every time I saw Aunt Macy she looked younger and happier. That day she was breezy and tan in a mint-green linen pantsuit, her hand locked in Edwin's. As I listened to her bubbling about a Hawaiian cruise they'd recently taken, I knew I'd done the right thing by bowing out of their lives when I did.

Aunt Macy and Edwin were my first formal guests since we'd moved into the house. Chad's family popped in from time to time—usually uninvited—and Mindy and her kids were always over, but Aunt Macy and Edwin were my first call-ahead-of-time visitors. I had made a pineapple upside down cake, which turned out to be one of my better efforts. With practice, my cooking skills had vastly improved since Chad and I were first married. I served the cake on new daisy-patterned Corelle dishes

Chad had bought me for Christmas, and I'd found some daisy paper napkins at the Dollar Store that coordinated perfectly.

I handed Aunt Macy a piece of cake I'd chosen especially for her, because it had a full ring of pineapple with a cherry in the center. As I gave her a napkin, all of a sudden, a secret from my past so embarrassing I'd never told a soul, came back to me. My eyes met with hers, and then we both glanced at the napkin, and then back at each other again. I knew we were thinking the same thing. My face became hot and I returned to that night, sitting in her bathroom with a piece of toilet paper dangling from my mouth. At the time, I didn't know the reason I ate toilet paper was because I had pica, a disorder caused from a mineral deficiency as a result of my poor diet. Now, even knowing it was not my fault, I would still have been mortified if anyone else found out. Aunt Macy was such an open, impulsive type; I was afraid she might innocently mention my stint as a goat to give everyone a good laugh. When she opened her mouth to speak, I held my breath.

"Doesn't this cake look delicious?" she said. "And daisy napkins to match the plates! Nice touch Tuesday Leigh!" Then she winked at me, letting me know our secret was just that—*our secret*. I exhaled and winked back.

When Edwin announced they needed to get on the road, my heart sank, because I didn't want them to leave. Right before they walked out the door, Aunt Macy took me aside to talk. "I wasn't going to tell you this," she said under her breath. "But I've changed my mind, because I realize you're a grown woman now, and I shouldn't keep things from you to protect you anymore. You have a right to know, so you can make up your own mind what to do."

"What is it, Aunt Macy. Is there something wrong?"

"Oh no, everything's fine. It's just that your mama called me the other day to try to get your phone number."

"Did you give it to her?"

"Of course not, I'd ever do that. I wasn't even going to tell you because I honestly believe you're happier without her meddling in your life."

"Did she say why she wanted my number after all this time?"

"Yes, apparently her family is having a reunion in August and she wants you to come. Personally I think she only wants you there to look better in front of her family. You know, still pretending as if nothing ever happened."

"Yeah, makes sense."

"I told her about your kids and she didn't seem too happy about the idea of being a grandmother. You know how your mama is. Anyway I said I'd tell you, but not to expect you to come. But you can make up your own mind what you want to do. Her number is the same if you want to call her."

"No, you're right Aunt Macy; I'd best stay away from her."

"Well it's for you to decide. Now give me a hug, because I've got to get on out of here before Edwin pulls out without me." I hugged her a little too tightly, a little too long. We both had tears in our eyes when she walked out the door.

After they left, I told Chad that Mama wanted us to come to a family reunion.

Big Mistake.

"We should go," he said.

"We should go? Haven't you heard anything I've told you about what she did to me?"

"Yeah, I know, but she's still the kids' grandmother. And just because she was mean to you doesn't mean she's going to be mean to them. You said she treated your brothers okay."

I hated how flippant he and his family were about my abuse. They gave me the impression—assuming they believed me at all—that it had somehow been my fault. Or that maybe things hadn't been as bad as I'd let on, and I should let bygones be bygones. "After all," Bobbi had said. "She's your mother; she brought you into this world. Family should forgive family, no matter what they've done." Neither Bobbi nor Chad understood how my childhood abuse had broken my heart and my spirit, and they probably never would. They had no idea what Mama was capable of, or why I didn't want my kids anywhere near her.

"I don't think I can stand to be around her," I said.

"Ah, come on, it'll only be for an hour or so. I want to meet this crazy lady myself." He turned to Molly, who'd just come in from playing. Do you want to go to a picnic and meet your other grandma?"

"Yeah!" Molly said, jumping up and down.

"Now you've done it," I growled.

"Baby, you know I wouldn't let anyone hurt you or the kids; I'd kill that crazy bitch if she ever laid a hand on you again."

When he said that, I softened up some. "I'll think about it," I said.

But the truth was, whether or not we were attending the family reunion was no longer up for debate, because now, thanks to Chad's big mouth, Molly thought she was going to a "picnic" to meet her "other grandma." Molly couldn't understand that seeing Mama would be no picnic, and her other grandmother was nothing like Bobbi. Bobbi wasn't without her faults, and God knows we had our share of differences, but she had proven to be a loving, attentive grandmother, and Molly adored her. The other grandmother, to ease her own guilt, would make a brief appearance in our life, and then disappear, leaving behind a trail of disappointment and confusion.

There was, however, a positive side to seeing Mama. It would give me the chance to prove to her I had found happiness, and contrary to what she'd said repeatedly when I was a child, I *could* find someone to love me. But most of all, it would give me the opportunity to show her—no, rub her nose in—Molly's beauty. And consciously, even though I didn't acknowledge I needed Mama, on a subconscious level, I missed, not so much her, but the fantasy mother, the mother I'd lost, or never really had. Although I didn't want to see her, a part of me romanticized the notion of the one in a million possibility of a mother-daughter reunion. We would make up, embrace, and become the best of friends. Once a week, we would meet for lunch and then go shopping. We'd call each other for recipes. I'd cry to her when Chad and I got into a fight, and she would always side with me, because that's what real mothers do.

The following day, I called Mama and told her we would be attending the reunion. She said it was going to be at my grandmother's—her mother's—house in Franklin Tennessee, on August 5th. She acted thrilled we were coming, and said since I had called long distance, we would catch up at the picnic. When I hung up the phone, as always after speaking with her, I was left with the perplexing impression we had shared completely different pasts.

The night before the reunion I didn't sleep at all. I stayed up planning how I would act in front of Mama, what I would wear, what I would say. For hours, I stood before a mirror rehearsing clever lines and practicing my smile. *Smiling is a good idea,* I decided. I would make sure I smiled often in her presence, an effortless smile, as if my happiness ran far below the surface.

In the car on the way to Tennessee, I couldn't sit still in my seat. I kept flipping down the mirror on the sun visor to check my make-up. I thought I looked fat in the shorts I had on, which I'd selected only minutes before we left, after trying on and rejecting everything else in my closet. I still hadn't lost all the weight I'd gained carrying Daryl.

At least twice, I told Chad to turn around and go home so I could change clothes, but he kept driving.

When we arrived at my grandmother's house, on wobbly legs, and in some sort of a self-induced trance, I followed Chad as he made his way to the backyard where everyone was congregated. A soon as we rounded the corner of the house, Mama descended upon us like a used car salesman on double commission day. It had been over five years since I'd last seen her, but she hadn't changed much. She was on the thinner side of the thirty pounds she had constantly gained and lost over the years. She had on white pants, and a boxy, kelly-green paisley shirt that looked like a large scarf folded in half. She'd lightened her hair and she still wore it curly and snug to her head. Now in her fifties, she appeared to be aging well. She went straight for Molly, who was beside me holding my hand. "What a pretty little girl!" she said.

"This is Molly," I said. "She turned five in June." Molly buried her face in my hip. "Say hello to your, grandma, honey."

"Hello, Molly!" Mama bent down. "Were you named after Molly Ringwald? I'll bet you were…"

"No," I interjected. "She *wasn't.*"

"Well, she's much prettier than Molly Ringwald anyway."

I forced a smile. "Say thank you!" I said, talking through Molly like I was a ventriloquist and she was my perfect little dummy.

Mama turned to Daryl, who was on Chad's hip, and took hold of one of his chubby arms. "And this must be the newest addition." Daryl retrieved his arm and put his head on Chad's shoulder.

"His name's Daryl," Chad said. "He's kinda shy."

"Darling!" Mama cooed. "He favors Ryan when he was that age." She turned to me, and I knew she wanted me to introduce her to Chad.

"Mama, this is my husband, Chad." *Did I linger long enough on the word husband?*

She slipped into her sexy voice, the one she always used when she was in the presence of a man. "*Chad,* so nice to meet you," she drawled. "You're a handsome cuss, yourself. Molly looks just like her Daddy!"

Chad grinned, and I wanted to elbow him in the ribs.

"So Ladybug, you're all grown up now with your own family! How ya like married life?"

The last time I'd seen Mama I'd gone off on her telling her I never wanted to lay eyes on her again until she was ready to fess up to what she'd done to me. Five years later, I was still pissed at her, because I could see she was playing the same old game of charades. But standing in front of her now, I didn't have the guts to pick up where I'd left off at Shoney's. Even though I knew she could no longer harm me, and if I wanted to I could beat her to a pulp, I froze up the minute she began to talk to me. I searched my mind for the clever comebacks I'd rehearsed the previous night, but like an etch-a-sketch someone had just shaken, all the thoughts that were so clear earlier in the car were now scattered in a million pieces in my head. "I love it!" I said, and managed to eke out one of the effortless smiles I'd practiced. "Tell Grandma we have to go to the bathroom now," I said through Molly, while tugging at her arm and pulling her toward the house.

"Oh, no, no, no, that will never do," said Mama. She looked at Chad and winked. "Do I look like a *grandma*?" She turned back to Molly. "Hon, you can call me Mama Rose."

The way she looked at Molly made me uneasy. The coldness in her eyes didn't match her phony smile. And Molly was acting strange too. For weeks, all she'd talked about was meeting her new grandma. Now that it was actually happening, she clamped onto my leg and wouldn't even look at Mama.

After Molly had used the bathroom, we came back out into the yard. On the way, I ran into Jimmy D., but we talked only a few minutes. He was still uncomfortable being friendly with me around Mama. My younger brother, Ryan, was there too. We spoke to each other, but nothing more. Across the yard, Mama was still talking to Chad, giggling and touching his shoulder. I couldn't stomach anymore of her flirting with my husband, so to pass the time, I carried on superficial conversations with a few of my relatives. Despite the sugary words they fed to me, I couldn't quite clear my palate of the bitterness their refusal to help me as a child had left in my mouth. I had, however, been looking forward to seeing my cousin, Eva who, at a Fourth of July family picnic had smuggled cookies from the kitchen for me. I was told she could not attend the reunion for reasons that were unclear, but her brother, Bruce was there.

"I'm glad you're doing okay," he said. "You had a rough way to go when you were a kid, didn't you?"

"Yeah, I guess you could say that."

"I want you to know that over the years, I've discussed how Aunt Rose treated you with my parents. Dad still regrets not doing anything to help you. He said there were many family arguments about it. Your dad protected Aunt Rose, you know, which made it much harder for my dad to do anything."

"Hmm, that's the first I've heard about anyone on Mama's side of the family even acknowledging my abuse, let alone attempting to do something about it. Thanks for telling me, Bruce; it helps to know somebody at least tried."

I chatted briefly with my grandmother, who we called "Mother" because she, like Mama, didn't like the idea of being a grandmother. She acted as though she hardly knew me, as she sipped Catawba wine from a red Solo cup.

Mama approached us. "My Ladybug's grown in to such a beautiful young woman, hasn't she Mother?" she said. Then she tilted her head downward, gazing woefully at the ground. "Just wish she'd come to see her mama once in a while." As if I, the cruel estranged daughter, was the reason we didn't have a relationship. To keep from tearing into her again, I got up and walked away.

After I'd picked at a plate of fried chicken and potato salad, I was ready to go home, so were the kids, and Chad had finally had enough of Mama too. After only being there one hour, we said our good-byes and headed for the car.

"I'll call you," Mama shouted out as we walked off. But I knew she wouldn't call, and I didn't want her to anyway.

"So what do you think?" I asked Chad, as we got back on the road.

"Looney Tunes," he said. "Crazy, but in a funny way."

"Funny? What do you mean by that?"

"I mean she doesn't have a clue how ridiculous she is. All the overacting about how wonderful you are, and then she gives you a mean look behind your back. And flirting with someone half her age? She actually thinks everybody's buying her bullshit; that's what makes her so funny. I started to call her out when she gave you that mean look, but I didn't want to cause any trouble."

"You would have done that for me?"

"Damn straight! I'm on your side."

"Thanks honey," I said. "So, do you believe what I told you about my childhood now?"

"I always believed you, but now I *really* believe you. That woman's a real basket case and I'm sure she's capable of just about anything."

To see Mama—to be reminded she was never going to change—reopened old wounds that had begun to scab over. Still, I was glad we went to the reunion because it served to quell any lingering delusion I had of having a normal relationship with her. No matter how hard she tried to play mother, I would never be able to place her in that role in my mind, or in my heart.

Most days it took a steady effort to keep my thoughts occupied so I wouldn't turn down the dark corridors leading back to my past. But every now and then, when I wasn't paying attention, I stumbled and fell, and suddenly found myself there.

After seeing Mama, I knew I'd be more vulnerable, so the day after the reunion I tried to stay busy. I cleared out all the kitchen cabinets and drawers, scrubbed them down with Pine-sol, and then put in new shelf liner. I did the same in the bathroom. Then I shampooed all the carpets in the house, using Glory and a sponge mop. When I'd finished, I still had a couple of hours left before I had to start supper. Molly was playing with Joey at his house, and Daryl was down for a nap, so I decided to mow the grass in the backyard.

I should have known better. The mindless work, the drone of the lawnmower, left too much available white space in my head. While my gaze was fixed on the tufts of grass being devoured by the mower, my mind escaped my control.

Daddy, Mama, my brothers and I are on some sort of family vacation. "It's good for us to get away after all that's happened," Daddy says to Mama. I know he means Audrey's death and Mama's accident. We're in a cave—Mammoth Cave comes to mind—winding single file through a tight, rocky pathway. We pass a sign that reads "Fat Man's Squeeze," and make our way to a vast open area of the cave. Ahead I can see a swinging bridge crudely made of wood and rope. Daddy reads a plaque on a podium at the entrance to the bridge. "Ooh, it's a bottomless pit!" he says. My imagination takes off. A bottomless pit? Does that mean if you fell in you would spin and tumble forever and never hit ground? Or is there a bottom after all, with dusty bones and snakes writhing in and out of skulls, but no one has made it out alive to tell? Daddy steps onto the bridge first, followed by the boys, then Mama and me. The cave is dark, the bridge, wobbly. Daddy and the boys continue to the other side, but Mama stops me in the middle. "This is where it happens" she whispers. "I'm going to push you over and everyone will think you fell." I clutch the ropes and start screaming at the top of my lungs. Mama jerks my arm and pulls me to the other end of the bridge. "I was just kidding, Weasel," she says. "Quit making a scene!"

This was a memory I'd never had before. Usually I recalled episodes of abuse in vivid detail. This one came back to me in blurry snapshots, as if I were watching it happen from across a smoke-filled room. I turned off the mower, walked around to the side of the house and sat on the steps in front of the door to collect my thoughts.

This new memory explained my mysterious fear of heights. Why every time I'd gone up the escalator when Aunt Macy took me to the mall, my stomach flopped over and my scalp got prickly. But why was it coming to me *now* after all this time? And why had I repressed it? Mama had done worse things to me that I had no trouble remembering. In the past the ghosts from my childhood had been resurrected by a related incident of abuse. Like whenever I went swimming, and the water crept up around my neck, a sudden sense of suffocation descended upon me and took me back to when Mama held my head under bathwater. But there was no correlation between the incident in the cave and mowing the grass. This disturbed me, because I'd worked hard to identify what situations triggered the bad memories, and took every precaution to avoid them. Even more disturbing was the chance that there were more of these shrouded ghosts haunting my subconscious, lying in wait for an opportunity to catch me off guard again.

Weeks passed, and Mama never called like she said she would. I wasn't surprised that she didn't make the effort to reenter my life, or ask to become a part of my kids' future. Molly and Daryl might have formed a bond with her only to be crushed when she inevitably disappeared. Once the kids had met their "other grandmother," I thought they might, at some point, want to go and visit her, and I prepared myself to deal with the possibility, but they never mentioned her again.

A month or so after the reunion, we started to get recurring late night phone calls. Whenever Chad answered the phone, the caller hung up, but when I picked up the line, a female voice on the other end said she was having an affair with Chad, and that I should leave him right away. "He's only with you for the kids," said the voice, faint and muffled. "When we're together, he tells me you're ugly and that he never loved you. He only married you because he felt sorry for you."

When I confronted Chad, he swore he was innocent, but I didn't believe him. "Then why is this person saying she's having an affair with you? Why would somebody even do that?"

"Hell if I know! There are all kinds of nut jobs out there. It's probably a prank call."

"A prank call *every* night?"

Chad became so aggravated with the calls, the next time we got one he went into the kitchen and picked up the second phone so he could listen in. "It's your mother, Tuesday! Don't you recognize her voice?" he blurted into the phone, laughing. "Hey Rose, how ya doing?"

The caller hung up.

When I came back to bed, Chad said, "I can't believe you couldn't tell it was your crazy mother. I'd know her drawl anywhere."

He was right; of course Mama was the mysterious mistress. It made perfect sense. She was still trying to destroy my life. Why would anything be different because I was grown? The breathy voice, the exaggerated southern drawl, had sounded familiar, but I didn't want to believe my mother would do that to me after all she had already put me through. We changed our phone number and made it unlisted and the calls stopped.

After that incident, my feelings toward Mama vanished completely. I was no longer hurt, or sad or even angry—I was nothing at all. I turned my emotions for her off to protect what was left of my battered heart. I made the decision to continue to stay as far away from her as I possibly could.

SAVING EMMA

THE DAY HAD come for Molly to start kindergarten. She was dressed in a new pink Henley and a pair of jeans with glittery stars on the back pockets. I put her hair in a high pony-tail and tied it with a pink ribbon. Her backpack bulged with crayons, Elmer's glue and construction paper. She was ready for her first day of school.

But I wasn't. Like any mother, I was sad and anxious about my baby's first step to independence. Molly wasn't nervous at all, even as she walked into her classroom. Confidence was one thing she had taken away from the pageants. She'd become fearless and feisty and eager to face the world—not at all like her mother. I prayed no one would ever rob her of that fiery spirit. A surge of panic rose from my chest when she turned around and waved at Daryl and me standing in the hall of the school. I knew it was my cue to leave.

A cheap plot of land became available in the rural area where Chad's mom and dad lived, and Chad jumped on it with all fours. He still despised the subdivision. He didn't like neighbors and complained about having to drive too far to do his hunting and fishing. The kids were excited about moving, and I loved the idea of a new house in the country, but cringed at the thought of living so close to Bobbi and Big Chad again.

The next thing I knew, we had a for sale sign on the front lawn and prospective buyers were traipsing in and out of our home. In less than four months the house sold to a single state trooper. As soon as we closed the deal, early that spring, we borrowed the money to start building on the land. We couldn't afford much square footage, so we chose an open plan with a vaulted ceiling to give the house an illusion of spaciousness.

We took our full sixty days to move out, because we barely had the foundation of our new house laid. When our sixty days were up, we had to put all our furniture in storage and rent an apartment in an old building downtown until we'd finished the house. The apartment was a cramped place with a cracked vinyl sofa and dingy shag carpet of a color I couldn't identify. It smelled of mildew and had a roach problem, but it was the only thing we could find that worked into our budget and didn't require us to sign a lease.

The next several months of the four of us crammed into that dank apartment crept by. When we'd finally finished the house and were able to move in, Chad got busy working on the yard, and I became engrossed in decorating the inside in a cozy country style. Soon our new house took on our family's personality and felt like a home.

My secret fear of driving and getting lost kept me manacled to the house. At one time, I had blamed Chad for my isolation, but now the blame could be placed nowhere but on me. He still didn't like the idea of me going places without him, but he wasn't nearly as bad as he'd once been. He had bought an old truck to drive to work, so the car was always available to me in case I needed to go somewhere.

When we lived in the subdivision, keeping my fear of driving concealed was easier with Mindy willing to drive me anywhere I needed to go. She'd even driven Molly to kindergarten, pointing out there was no reason for me to get Daryl out when she had to drive Joey to the school anyway. To try to do my part, sometimes I picked the kids up in the afternoon, but not without trembling the whole way. Molly now rode the bus to school, so I didn't have to worry about that anymore, but I lived in constant dread that she or Daryl would get sick, or be hurt, when Chad wasn't there and I wouldn't be able to drive them to the emergency room.

Mindy's driving me around wasn't the only thing I missed about her. I missed *her*. We had become close like sisters. We still talked over the phone a couple of times a week, and I saw her on volleyball nights, but it wasn't the same as always having her near. Molly missed her friends in the old neighborhood too, but with her bubbly personality, it didn't take her long to make friends with a girl her age that lived next door.

Molly's new friend was a frail and timid blond named Emma. She reminded me of myself at her age, so I was instantly drawn to her, but I could hardly get her to talk to me, except to say hi. The only time she seemed to open up was when she and Molly were playing.

Emma spent quite a bit of time at our house. She came in with Molly every day when they got off the school bus and often stayed until dark. On the weekends, she sometimes showed up at our door early in the morning, and then stayed all day, eating both lunch and supper with us. Molly adored Emma, and I didn't mind her being around, because she was a well-behaved kid, but I found it odd that her parents didn't want her home more. I became suspicious of this and started asking questions.

"Emma, is it okay with your parents that you're over here so much?"

"Yes," she said, staring at her feet.

"I just thought maybe they missed you."

"My daddy's at work and my mommy don't care; she's always asleep."

"Why is your mommy always asleep?"

"She's tired."

Molly tugged at Emma's arm, "Come on, Emma; let's go in my room."

When I realized I wasn't going to get much out of Emma, I decided to investigate on my own. That night, after supper, I started by finding out if Chad knew anything about Emma's parents.

"Do you know Emma's dad," I asked him, casually.

"Yeah, he works in the mines."

"Does he seem nice?"

"I guess; he's just a regular guy."

"What about her mother? Do you know her?"

"Yeah, we went out a few times in school."

"So you know her better, right?"

"Right, but not much; we didn't go out like *that*."

"What do you mean?"

He grinned. "I mean we didn't talk that much."

"Oh. Well did she *seem* normal to you?"

"Normal? Hell, I don't know! Why?"

"Because Emma told me she sleeps a lot."

"So? What are you getting at?"

"I think it's weird that Emma is over here so much."

"Why don't you ask Emma why she's over here so much?"

"I hate to do that. I'm afraid I'll embarrass her."

"Well, you're barking up the wrong tree here."

The next afternoon when Emma got off the school bus, I noticed she had a couple of bruises on one of her legs. I stooped down to her. "Honey what happened to your leg?"

"I don't know," she mumbled, still not making eye contact.

"Did someone hit you?"

"I don't think so."

I took her by the shoulders. "Emma, look at me. Did your mommy or daddy whip you there?"

She started to cry. "No! My mommy and daddy don't whip me!"

"Are you sure?"

"Mama, leave Emma alone!" Molly interjected. "You're scaring her!"

152

Molly was right. To Emma, I was a woman she barely knew grabbing her by the shoulders demanding answers. "Oh, Emma, honey, I'm so sorry," I said, turning loose of her. Molly took Emma's hand and they went out to play.

Emma's reaction to my questions aroused my suspicions even more. I was convinced something was going on in her house. When Chad got in from work, I told him what had happened.

"I think Emma is being abused."

"What makes you think that?" he asked.

"She has bruises on her legs."

"So does Molly. Kids fall."

"She started crying when I asked her if her parents whipped her."

"You probably scared the shit out of her! Leave the kid alone!"

"I can't just stand by and let her be mistreated!"

"Tuesday, every time we go to the grocery store and you see a mother spanking her kid you cry abuse. I'm sick of hearing it! Nobody's being abused, so drop the subject and don't bring it up again!"

"I saw her run into her daddy's arms when he got home from work the other day, so I think it's her mother" I said. "I could at least call social services."

"Yeah and what if you're wrong. You'll disrupt their family and Emma won't be able to play with Molly anymore because we'll be their enemies for life."

"But what if I'm right?"

"You're not. Mind your own business, Tuesday."

What does he know? I thought. Even though he denied it, I suspected he still had his doubts about my abuse.

That night, I lay awake in bed thinking about Emma and how I could save her. *If she is being abused, I of all people should do something.* But Chad was right about one thing; I couldn't report Emma's mother without proof of abuse. I made up my mind to go to Emma's house the next day and meet her mother. We lived right next door to one another and our kids played together. *It's the neighborly thing to do.*

The following morning, I readied myself to visit Emma's mother. I baked oatmeal cookies to take with me. I was sitting at the kitchen table trying to get my nerve up, when the doorbell rang. The doorbell never rang. *It must be Bobbi.*

I opened the front door to a small-boned blond woman in what appeared to be a nurse's uniform. "Hi," she said. "I'm Amy from next door; Emma's mom."

"Oh… hi. I'm Tuesday. You're not going to believe this, but I was getting ready to come over to *your* house!"

"That's so funny!" she said. She had a sweet smile. But that didn't mean anything; Mama appeared to be nice too. "I thought it was time we meet each other since our girls play together."

"Me too; come in."

"Okay, I'll step in for a minute, but I can't stay long." She walked in and stood by the door.

"So, you're a nurse?"

"Uh-huh. I work third shift at the hospital. I just got off." *Mama was a nurse,* I thought. Amy looked around her at everything but me. *Was she nervous, or just shy, like Emma?* "Your house is so pretty!" she said.

"Thanks. Would you like some coffee?"

"Oh, no, I've got to get to sleep so I can wake up when Emma gets home from school."

"Emma told me you sleep a lot."

"Sometimes I'm still asleep when she gets home. She used to wake me up, but lately all she wants to do is play with Molly!"

"Molly loves playing with her too. Seems like she's always here!"

Amy's face turned pink. She was a mood ring person—someone so pale-skinned her complexion color changed with her emotions. "Emma's not getting on your nerves is she?" she asked.

"No, not at all!"

"Because if she is, let me know and I'll keep her home."

"Emma's a good kid. I don't mind having her around."

"The thing is Molly's the first real friend Emma's ever had. She's so introverted. She gets it from me." Her blush deepened. "Molly has brought her out of her shell and I am so thankful for that."

From years of watching Mama deceive everyone around her, I knew good acting when I saw it. Amy was not an abusive parent. She was a loving mother concerned about her daughter's problem with shyness.

"I'm glad the girls are friends," I said, in a softer voice than before. "It's good for both of them."

Amy turned for the door. "I've got to get to sleep before I fall over. So nice to meet you, Tuesday, and if you ever need anyone to watch Molly, you let me know."

"Thanks, and nice to have met you too," I said. "Amy wait," I called out to her as she walked away. I jogged into the kitchen and got the cookies. "I made these for you. I hope you like oatmeal raisin cookies."

"My favorite! Thank you! You're so sweet!"

After she'd left I hung my head in shame. Chad was right; I saw child abuse where there wasn't any. Amy was a nice, hard working lady, doing the best she could as a mother. If Chad hadn't stopped me, I might have turned her in to the social services, and possibly ruined her life. I thought about my neighbors growing up, and wondered if maybe they had felt the same way.

HUNGRY AGAIN

A S AN ADULT who'd been starved as a child, I considered eating a luxury and a privilege. Because of this mindset, I often overindulged. But somehow I'd always managed to keep my weight under control, until I became pregnant with Daryl and put on close to sixty pounds. Almost three years later, I still hadn't lost all the extra weight.

One day, I nonchalantly mentioned to Chad that I needed to go on a diet.

"That's probably a good idea," he responded a little too quickly. "You *are* beginning to look like a giant bottle."

A normal woman with healthy self-esteem might have ignored what Chad said, or come back at him with a clever counter punch. But I was in no aspect normal. Not even close. His words had cut straight to my heart, and inside, I was screaming hysterically—a very abnormal reaction. But I could do a good impersonation of normal. I'd learned how through watching TV and observing the people around me.

"Go to hell, Chad." I said, with an I-couldn't-care-less-what-people-think laugh. I was so convincing, he never knew the depth of the wound he had inflicted, and he would never know. In bed, after he went to sleep, I muffled my sobbing with my pillow.

The next day I started my diet. I didn't adhere to any specific regimen, like the Atkins plan, or the then popular Grapefruit Diet, but rather one I'd created on my own. It was called the Eat Practically Nothing Diet.

Food had become such an important part of my life, it took great effort to adjust to my new eating habits. The first few days of my diet messed with my head more than my stomach, taking me back to the days when food was scarce. But losing the weight was a priority, a mission—my new obsession—and I'd swore not to stop until I was satisfied. The problem was I had not yet defined *satisfied*.

When I started a new obsession, I went all in. I talked Chad into buying me some scales and a book to educate myself on calories and fat grams. I studied the book until I could accurately cite the calories per serving of almost any food. I kept a meticulous mental record of my daily caloric intake, making sure it stayed around 1,200. I had learned from my reading that in order to lose weight, total fat consumed should never exceed three grams per every 100 calories. At any point during a day I knew, not only how many calories I'd taken in, but also how many grams of fat.

Soon food lost its appeal. What had once been a deity I worshipped had now become my enemy. Numbers were constantly whirling around in my head. Every morning I woke up planning what I would eat that day. At night, I lay in bed unable to sleep for calculating my calories and fat grams, double checking to make sure I hadn't exceeded my daily allotment. If I determined that I'd gone even one calorie over the set amount, I would get up out of bed in the middle of the night and sprint up and down the stairs—sometimes for more than an hour—until I was sure I had burned the extra calories.

For the first couple of months, I lost weight at a steady pace. Then my body adjusted to the diet and my weight loss slowed down. I cut my daily caloric intake to 1,000 and increased the intensity of my exercise routine. I started jumping rope, doing pushups, and lifting weights two or three times a day for an hour each session.

Chad began to complain about my preoccupation with exercising and compulsive weighing, claiming I was neglecting him and the kids. To get him off of my back, I stopped working out while he was home. But I snuck in exercise at night, like running in place when I went to the bathroom, or doing quick laps around the yard when I took out the trash.

Soon the weight started to drop rapidly from my five feet seven inch frame. The first thing in the morning I stepped on the scales. It was exciting to see the needle inch down a little more every day. Fat continued to melt away right before my eyes, until my weight had plummeted from 150 to 105 pounds. I weighed 120 before I got pregnant with Daryl, but I had no intention of returning to my former size. I loved my slender new body, how my once binding jeans now hung loosely on my protruding hipbones. But most gratifying of all, losing weight was something *I* made happen—something *I* controlled.

By accident, I discovered a way to expedite my weight loss even more. Ever since I had Daryl I'd been prone to constipation, so I decided to try a laxative. I followed the package directions of a dosage of two pills. Nothing happened, but some cramping, so I took two more pills, and finally got results. Afterward, I noticed my belly had gone from flat to concave. I got on the scales and saw I'd lost two pounds. This got me to thinking. *If four pills made me lose two pounds then maybe eight will make me lose four or five.*

After months of dieting, exercise, and laxatives, my period suddenly stopped. I knew I couldn't be pregnant, because I'd had my tubes tied after Daryl was born. I told Mindy, and she said she'd heard about a woman who'd had a tubal and still got pregnant because her tubes grew back together. This scared me, but not enough to make me go to the doctor. I was positive I wasn't pregnant because I didn't have any other symptoms, and after two children, I knew how my body responded to pregnancy.

A few weeks later, my hair started falling out by the fistfuls. I decided it was time to go get checked out. The doctor examined me and ran a few tests, and determined I'd stopped my period because I hardly had any body fat. He said my fat to muscle ratio was like that of a teen gymnast, not a woman in her twenties. I was okay with not having any more periods, but according to the doctor, the hormonal imbalance from my dieting could cause other problems besides not having a period, one of them being hair loss. He told me I needed to get my weight up to 118 pounds to resume my period and stabilize my hormone level. The thought of gaining even one ounce terrified me, let alone almost eighteen pounds, but my fear of losing my hair was greater than my fear of being fat, so I had no other option.

To gain weight, I ate only the blandest foods that lay heavy in my mouth, like rice and dry toast. I would not allow myself to taste, because I didn't want my old lover to woo me into his arms again. It took months, but eventually I gained back some of the weight I'd lost, resumed my menstrual cycle, and most important of all, I stopped losing my hair.

But just because my body was back to normal didn't mean I had to abandon my control over it. I got better at concealing my dieting and exercise, and continued to keep a close check on the scales, never allowing my weight to get one ounce over 118 pounds, which the doctor claimed was still too thin for a woman of my height. My life became a silent daily struggle to keep from breaking through the fragile membrane between merely watching my weight and returning to a full blown eating disorder.

ECHOES OF DISCONTENTMENT

AFTER MY WEIGHT had stabilized, Chad asked Bobbi to watch the kids while he took me to buy some new clothes that fit properly. There weren't many places to shop in Sullivan, but Mindy had told me about a trendy ladies clothing store that had recently opened downtown, called Ashley's.

Ashley's had a good selection of stylish clothes, and I found two tops and a pair of shorts at a price Chad was willing to pay. While we were checking out, the sales clerk, a chatty fresh-faced woman around my age, mentioned, in passing, that if I knew of anyone who needed a job they were hiring.

"I'd love to work in a place like this," I said.

"Why don't you put in your application then?"

I glanced at Chad. He shook his head, *no.* "You already have a job—taking care of the house and kids."

"But Chad, both Molly and Daryl are in school now. I could work during the day before they get home."

"It would only be part-time," the clerk pointed out.

Chad ignored her comment. She pulled a sheet of paper from under the counter and gave it to me. "Here, take an application anyway in case you change your mind."

As soon as we were in the car, I started in on Chad. "I would just like to have my own money so I don't have to ask you every time I need to buy tampons."

"My money *is* your money; it's *our* money."

"You say that but it doesn't seem that way to me."

Over the next couple of days, I chinked away at Chad's resistance, until I'd talked him in to letting me apply for the job at Ashley's. "I probably won't get it anyway," I told him. "I have no experience at all in retail."

The next morning, I filled out the application, listing my high school creative writing teacher and Mindy as references. When I had finished, I looked over what I'd written and became convinced I wouldn't get the job. I remembered thinking the same thing when I saw the crowd of teenagers interviewing for the cashier position at McDonald's. But this was a much better job that paid over minimum wage, with a store discount and everything. Still I tried to stay positive. *Maybe I'll get lucky; maybe no one else will apply and they'll have to give it to me.*

I wanted to get the application to the store before Chad had a chance to change his mind, which meant I had to take it there while he was at work, which meant I would have to deliver it myself. Confronted with my fear of driving, I reconsidered my decision to apply for the position. *How am I supposed to hold a job at Ashley's when I can't even muster enough courage to drive there and drop off the application?*

Fretting was getting me nowhere. I decided to move forward, to start getting ready to take the application to Ashley's without thinking. After I took a shower, I dressed in white pants and one of the new tops Chad had bought me. I put on mascara and pink lip gloss, and used a curling iron to shape the bangs of my long shag into perfect feathered wings. Then I grabbed the application, got in the car, and began backing out of the driveway as if driving was something I did every day.

When I pulled out onto the highway in front of our house, I stopped breathing. With the car still in reverse, I slammed both feet on the brake and began taking in quick, shallow breaths of air. Sitting there, with half the car in the road and half still in the driveway, it suddenly struck me that I could be plowed over by a coal truck. I shifted the car into gear to go back up the driveway toward the house, but right before I turned in, I hit the brake again. Getting a job was my chance to change the definition of who I was, to be something more than Chad's wife. While being a mother had nourished my soul like nothing else, now that the kids were both in school, I feared too much idle time would put me at the mercy of my memories. I fought off the impulse to pull back up to the house, and began slowly creeping forward on the highway.

As I drove, my heart raced and sweat from my armpits trickled down my sides. While my many other fears were an inconvenience, none of them had proven to be as debilitating as this one, threatening to rob me of the freedom and independence I now craved. I struggled to see the road through angry tears. I couldn't process the absurd anxiety driving brought on, or locate the source of my fear. Unlike my long list of other fears and phobias, it had no direct connection—of which I was conscious—to my childhood abuse.

Creeping along at a snail's pace, not only were my thoughts on the possibility of having a wreck, but also getting lost. I had no sense of direction. Starting when I was in junior high school, I lost my way in my day to day life on a regular basis. I had trouble finding my classrooms even after I'd been to them dozens of times. One year, when I was in high school, I lugged all my books with me to every class, because I couldn't find my assigned locker. The few times I'd driven Aunt Macy's car, before this new phobia set in, I used landmarks to locate where I had parked. As an adult, I often took the wrong turn coming out of the bathroom at restaurants, and found myself wandering aimlessly for several minutes waiting for Chad to come looking for me. But no one with half a brain got lost in Sullivan. The entire town was on one street and the highway in front of our house led directly to it. Even so, every now and then, when I looked along the roadside, my mind would trick itself into believing I had somehow landed in unknown territory.

The drive to Ashley's should have taken ten minutes, at the most, but for me it took an hour—or at least that's what it seemed like. When we got there, I couldn't go in right away because I was sweaty and shaky. With the air conditioner at full blast, I sat in the parking lot for a few minutes to get myself together. Then I refreshed my melted makeup, grabbed the job application from the seat beside me, and went inside.

When I walked in, a sales clerk out on the floor approached me and said hello. The woman who had sold me my clothes stood behind the counter. I could tell from the expression on her face she recognized me. "Hi, again," she said. "What are you shopping for today?"

"I didn't come to shop this time." I extended the application to her. "I came to drop this off."

"Great, we still have a position available." She glanced over the application. "Do you have time for an interview today?"

"I guess..."

"It won't take long; we'll just step in the back."

The friendly clerk's name was Becky, and she was the store manager. She asked me a few questions about why I wanted to work at Ashley's, and if I was hired, when I would be available to work. When we'd finished the interview, she told me I had the job if I wanted it. Walking to the car I was stunned. *What just happened?*

Filled with the excitement of the change to come, the trip home from Ashley's was much easier than the drive there had been. When I passed the Dairy Maid, I decided to go off my diet and treat myself to a soft-serve cone. It was an ice-cream kind of day.

That evening, over Chad's favorite meal of fried chicken livers and mashed potatoes, I told him I'd been hired at Ashley's. Even though he had said it was okay for me to apply, I could tell from his reaction he didn't think I would actually get the job.

He grabbed a slice of white bread from a stack in the center of the table and took an angry bite out of it. "My mom's not watching the kids while you work," he said.

"She won't have to. Becky's going to set up my schedule so I will only work while they're in school."

"Is *Becky* gonna cook my dinner too? Cause I'm not waiting until seven o'clock every night to eat."

"I'll make sure dinner is on the table by the time you get home."

"Well, if this house starts going to hell, you're quitting! You got that?"

"I can take care of the house and work too." I touched his arm. "I promise, Chad, everything will be fine; you'll never even know I'm gone."

He jerked his arm away. "Yeah, we'll see about that."

After dinner, Chad positioned himself in his usual place in front of the TV and sulked over his beer. Although he claimed to be concerned my job would cause me to start neglecting the kids and house, his insecurities ran much deeper. For the rest of the night, I stayed out of his way, because I knew if we started arguing it would be about more than my job.

Chad's fears were not unfounded. For the last few years, I'd been harboring a secret yearning to be free from the prison my marriage to him had become. I had been locked up as a child, and now, once again, I was shackled by Chad's controlling nature. Maybe if I had enjoyed a nurturing upbringing, from which I had gained the confidence to pursue a fulfilling young adulthood, a simple life like the one he was offering me, as a mother and homemaker, might have sufficed.

I was as much to blame for my predicament as Chad. Just as he'd known before we were married that I'd missed out on my childhood, I'd known about his jealous and controlling nature, and made the decision to build a life with him anyway. Maybe his promise of constraint was the very quality that made me love him. His control had felt familiar, and familiar felt safe. Even knowing there were better paths to take, I chose the one I knew, because the unknown was too threatening. And maybe my need for someone to take care of me was what had drawn Chad to me, made him feel more like a man.

With mature eyes, I could now see that what you want at twenty is not necessarily what you will need when you're thirty. For the first time in my life, I had a choice. With Chad's help, I could continue to seclude myself from the rest of the world, sinking deeper and deeper into the quicksand of isolation, or I could confront my fears, kill them, and trample over their dead bodies on my way to join the living.

All I wanted was a tiny slice of independence pie. For too long, I had sat quietly while everyone around me ate; now I wanted my fair share. And I thought I deserved it. For ten years, I had been a good redneck wife. I'd tolerated Chad's kooky, backward family, his excessive alcohol consumption and resulting drunken rampages. I had, on many occasions, watched, not only our kids, but also his sister's, when they went bar-hopping at night. I had done all the cooking and cleaning. I'd made his lunch every day, packed it in his bucket, and then when he got home washed the bucket, along with his crusty mining clothes. I'd even gone fishing with him and pretended as if I liked it. Except for a short time during the projectile vomiting phase of my pregnancy with Molly, I'd never turned him down when he asked for sex. Granted, in recent years, it had become robotic for both of us, still he got off.

In his defense, he had put up with a lot from me too: moodiness and a tendency to inertia, my obsessive behavior first with the pageants, then volleyball, and then exercising. He had provided for me and bought me everything he thought I needed. And he was willing to continue to do all this as long as he called the shots.

THE DARK STRANGER

THE FIRST FEW days of driving to work were stressful, and I sometimes had panic attacks along the way and had to pull over to the side of the road. But each day it got easier as I became familiar with my route, until eventually, I was fine as long as I went the same way every day.

As far as I was concerned, other than the driving, working at Ashley's slipped seamlessly into my life. Three days a week I went in at nine in the morning, and Becky let me off at two-thirty in the afternoon, so I'd be home before the kids got off the bus. On my days off, I cleaned and caught up on the laundry. It was a bit of a challenge to help the kids with their homework and have dinner ready before Chad got home, but well worth the trouble, because working kept my mind occupied and put a few dollars in my purse.

With each passing day, Chad became more resentful of my job. Sometimes I'd come home chattering about something funny that had gone on at work, or an interesting person I'd met, and you could almost see smoke coming out of his ears. He began picking at everything I did, and finding fault in my cooking and housecleaning, even though nothing had changed since I'd started working. Already struggling with insecurities, he sensed my longing for freedom and began holding on even tighter, not in a loving, affectionate way, but in a watching-me-like-a-hawk way. But I refused to allow his behavior to deter me. I clung to my job with every ounce of determination I had.

Besides the kids, my work was the one bright spot in my life. I enjoyed helping other women put together trendy outfits, and showing them how to accessorize with jewelry and scarves. To my surprise, I was good at it too. Becky was quick to praise my fashion sense and attentiveness to the customers. She began pushing for me to put in extra hours on nights and weekends. Although I wanted to work, because of Chad I had to turn her down.

Chad and I continued to go through the motions of marriage, doing all the usual things married people do, but my job had become a wedge between us. When we were home together, I kept busy and stayed away from him as much as I could. Ours was a problem I didn't want to address, because I knew solving it would mean I'd have to quit my job. Somehow we made it through a year this way. He did a lot of hunting and fishing, and my volleyball team joined another league and I began playing twice a week. He wanted me to quit my volleyball team too, but I refused. My newfound independence had taken on a life of its own since I'd discovered, aside from physically restraining me, Chad couldn't stop me from doing what I wanted.

It was around lunchtime, on one of the coldest days of the year. Business was slow at the store, so I decided to change the clothes of the mannequins in the front window. When I'd finished, and was stepping down from the platform, I noticed a couple of men outside walking down the sidewalk. The men stopped in front of the store, looked at me curiously for a minute, and then came inside.

Men rarely came into Ashley's, except on Christmas Eve when they frantically searched through the lingerie and blouses for gifts for their wives. They seemed lost as they thumbed clumsily through the racks, their eyes imploring me to tell them what to buy, in what size, and then wrap it up. I liked helping these men, because money wasn't an issue at such a dire time, and they usually bought whatever I suggested. They were a refreshing diversion from the women who took ten outfits into the dressing room, stayed in the store for hours, and then left without buying a thing.

While it was unusual for men to come into the store at all, men like the ones standing before me now *never* came in, even at Christmastime. Both of them, who appeared to be in their early forties, were dressed in expensive-looking suits, and top coats with tartan scarves draped around the collars. They both had spiky short black hair. The taller man had a neatly trimmed beard; the shorter, and more handsome one, was clean-shaven. Their shoes were shiny and stylish. Their fingernails were manicured better than mine, and they smelled better than me too.

I didn't even know there *were* such men in Sullivan. The local guys wore John Deer caps, Carhartt jackets, and Wrangler jeans with Scoal can rings on the back pockets. Their tee-shirts had sports logos and names of rock bands on them. Clearly the men before me were not coal miners, and most likely from out of town. They looked like Italian mafia men I'd once seen in a movie on TV.

"Hello. May I help you with something?" I asked.

"You may be able to," the short one said. He had a throaty accent I didn't recognize, but I was sure it wasn't Italian. It reminded me of a girl from India I worked with at McDonalds, but this man's skin was much lighter than hers. "I'm looking for a present for my wife."

"Do you have anything in particular in mind?"

"As a matter of fact I do. When we were at dinner the other night she saw another woman wearing a pair of pants she liked. They were leather and had zippers on the sides of the legs," he said, his *s's* and *z's* rolling from the back of his mouth. "Do you have anything like that here?"

"Were the zippers at the ankles?"

"No, they started at the hip and went to the ankle."

Why would anyone need zippers down both sides of her pants? Maybe she's a stripper. I was sure he was mistaken, but he was my customer and my job was to assist him. "No, I'm sorry; we don't have anything like that here.

Can I show you something else? We have pants with *stripes* on the sides."

"Stripes won't do; it has to be zippers." He glanced down at my feet. "I like the boots you have on though. Do you sell those here?"

I had on cream colored canvas knee boots that I'd bought at K-Mart. He'd probably never seen the inside of a K-Mart "No, I'm sorry, we don't sell shoes here."

"Shame; I suppose I'll have to shop for them elsewhere. Would you mind lifting your skirt a little so I can see them better?"

His request made me uncomfortable, and I debated whether or not I should do it. The simpler solution would have been to go ahead and honor his request, instead of trying to concoct a refusal that didn't come off as rude or presumptive, risking offending him and embarrassing myself as well. I scrutinized his softly rounded eyes that drooped down at the outer corners. They were kind eyes. And he *was* a married man. A married man who obviously loved his wife enough to buy her gifts.

"No, I don't mind at all," I said, as if it was no big deal, and lifted my long prairie-style skirt up to my knees so he could see the boots.

A smile appeared on his face revealing teeth so perfect they looked like dentures. "Lovely!" he said. "Yes, I'll definitely have to have those." I got the impression he wasn't talking about my boots.

"We need to get back to work," said the tall one, who had a similar accent. *They work around here?* My curiosity got the best of me. "Where do you work?"

"The Job Corps Center," replied the tall one.

"Really? My dad used to work there!"

"He did? Well where does he work now?" the shorter man asked.

"Nowhere; he was killed in a car accident almost fifteen years ago," I answered, glumly.

He touched my shoulder. "So sorry. What's your father's name?"

"Nick Storm; he was head of personnel."

"Yes, I've heard of him; he was well-liked and respected around the center."

"We've got to get back to work," insisted the taller man.

The short man glanced at his watch. "Wow, we really do." They both turned around and headed for the door. The short man waved as they walked out.

For the rest of the day, I thought about Daddy. The mornings he snuck to my bed to give me a hug and a kiss before he left for work. And the day the lady from social services came to the house, and how mad he'd been at me then. When I thought of the lies he told the social worker to cover for Mama it hurt so much I had to shake the thought from my head to keep from crying. I could see him loping away across the parking lot of the bus station after he dropped me off the day I left home. And the last time I saw him before he died, sitting on Aunt Macy's front porch, pleading with me to forgive him for not doing more to stop Mama's abuse of me. That was when he told me to marry a man who made me feel good about myself. With maturity, I'd realized the significance of his advice.

Daddy would never have approved of the husband I'd chosen. Chad was nothing like him—he had no college education, no ambition, and a tendency toward violence. And he definitely did *not* make me feel good about myself. That may have been one reason I married him—as an unconscious act of defiance against Daddy, because even after so many years the burn of his betrayal was still with me.

It was getting close to Christmas, and Becky had persuaded me to put in more hours at the store. In addition to working an extra day during the week, instead of getting off at two or two-thirty, I'd been staying until four-thirty or five.

Molly, now twelve, had been doing some light babysitting for family and friends, so she was responsible enough to keep an eye on Daryl for a few hours after school while I worked. A soon as I got off, I rushed home and slapped something together for dinner. As my job became more demanding of my time, our family meals became more processed. Lately we'd been eating a lot of Hamburger Helper and frozen pizzas. When I was off work, I tried to make a huge pot of soup or chili to keep from having to cook again for at least two days.

One afternoon, I got caught up with a customer, lost track of time and didn't get home until after Chad. When I drove up he and the kids were walking out of the house.

"Where are you guys going?" I asked.

"The kids are starving; we're going to Mom's for dinner."

Later on, when Molly and Daryl were asleep, everything came to a head.

"You're quitting that fucking job!" Chad screamed.

"Keep your voice down; you'll wake the kids."

"I'm tired of eating the slop you've been trying to pass off as dinner!"

"I'm not quitting!" I said defiantly.

"We don't need that piddly-ass money you make! You need to be here when the kids get home from school."

"I don't want to have to ask you for money when I want to buy something."

"What the hell do you need to buy?"

"Well, for one thing a Christmas present for you."

"I don't want anything for Christmas!" he said. "Now what do you need it for? Tampons? Tell you what. I'll pay you whatever you make a week working at Ashley's."

"I'm not quitting, Chad!"

"Oh yes you are, unless you want to be out on the streets!"

I broke out crying. "You can't just kick me out!"

"You'll change your mind about that when you come home one day and find out the locks have been changed on the door."

I knew he couldn't put me out on the streets, but he could make my life a living hell. "At least let me work through Christmas," I said.

"Okay, but go ahead and tell Becky tomorrow so she can be looking for somebody to take your place."

A few days later, around lunchtime, the man looking for the zippered pants came back into the store. *What could he possibly want now?* We didn't have the weird zippered pants. We didn't sell boots. I walked out onto the sales floor to greet him. "Hello again."

"Hello! I was so rude the other day, I didn't even introduce myself." He extended his hand. "My name is Mehmet Demir. But everyone calls me Matt."

That's definitely not Italian. I took his hand "Nice to meet you, Matt. I'm Tuesday Sutton."

"I also have a confession to make," he said. "I wasn't really looking for pants with zippers down the legs."

I knew it! I thought. *There aren't any pants like that.* "You weren't?"

"I made it all up so I would have an excuse to come in."

"Why would you do that?"

"I saw you in the store window and was so overtaken by your beauty I had to talk to you."

Overtaken by my beauty? I'd never had anyone say anything remotely like that to me before. As far as I knew the word, *beauty*, and a reference to me, had never before been used in the same sentence. Cute, yes; good looking, maybe once—but never beautiful. His intention—for whatever reason—was to compliment me, I knew that, and yet my reaction was the opposite. I felt like I was at the gynecologist and my legs were spread and up in stirrups.

I felt a blush coming on and I tried to ward it off. "Don't be silly."

"You're blushing!" Matt said "Why are you embarrassed? People must tell you you're beautiful all the time."

"No, not really." *Please, please don't talk about beauty anymore.* I steered our conversation in a different direction. "What about the boots?"

"I actually did like the boots. But I asked to see them hoping I would get a peek at your legs."

"You're kidding me!"

He bowed his head. "I know it was wrong and I apologize."

Never before had a man found me so attractive to lie to get to know me. Not even my husband. Definitely not my husband. If Chad thought I was beautiful he'd never voiced it. Sometimes I didn't want to have to *assume* I was desirable, like he expected me to. I wanted someone to tell me, but at the same time, hearing it from Matt made me nervous.

My legs were still up in stirrups, as my mind fumbled for something to say. "Is there something I can show you for your wife while you're in here?"

"Oh, no."

Did he make his wife up too? "You *do* have a wife. Don't you?"

"Yes, that part is true," he said, dismally, as if he were telling me about a bunion he couldn't get rid of. "But it's

179

a marriage only in name. It was sort of arranged by our parents."

Arranged? Where is he from? "If you don't mind my asking, what is your nationality?"

"Not at all. I was born in Turkey, but I've been an American citizen since I was eighteen."

Geography wasn't my best subject in school, but I was pretty sure Turkey was somewhere in the Middle East. "Oh, really?" I said.

"My wife and I have agreed to get a divorce," he continued. "But there hasn't been an urgency to file, so we decided to live in the same home in separate rooms. It's mostly for our son. He's ill—kidney disease."

"I'm sorry your son's sick."

"What about you? Are you married?"

"Yes. Ten years."

"Happily?"

"No." *Why did I say that*? It was a reflex—a hiccup. I was so pissed at Chad for making me quit my job, it slipped out. But I had no business telling a stranger about my personal life. I wanted to take it back. No sounded too absolute. There had been good times with Chad, and he was the father of my children.

Right about then, a regular customer walked into the store with her teenaged daughter. *Thank God.* "Well, Matt," I said, sales clerk politely. "It's been nice talking to you, but if there isn't anything I can show you I need to tend to the other customers."

"Yes, of course." He nodded his head twice and then left the store.

When he was gone, I was relieved because I couldn't bear to hear one more compliment. And yet, later, alone inside my head, I found myself recalling our conversation and wallowing in his words.

Several days later, Matt came into the store again. *Now what?* I thought when I saw him walk through the door.

Smiling, as if someone had just told him a joke, and with a confident swagger, he made his way through the racks of clothes to the counter where I was standing.

"Hello, Tuesday! How are you?"

"Hi Matt; I'm fine."

He chuckled. "She remembered my name!"

"Is there something I can help you with?"

"No, no, just came in to say hello to you. I woke up this morning and realized what day of the week it is, and thought of you, my beautiful friend, Tuesday."

Oh, no, not that beautiful crap again. "How nice of you."

"I was wondering if you might like to join me for lunch sometime."

Had he forgotten I was married? "Sweet of you to ask, but remember, I'm married."

"I know you're married. So am I. That doesn't mean we can't be friends. I like you better than anyone I've met in a long time. We both have unhappy marriages; I thought we could talk about it and maybe help each other."

Friends? I can't be friends with someone who thinks I'm beautiful. Besides, I knew Chad would never go for me having a male friend, particularly one who looked like Matt. He didn't even like the idea of me being friends with women. "No I really shouldn't; it wouldn't be right."

"Ah Tuesday, you're making more of this than is necessary. It's only lunch." He pressed his hands together as if he was getting ready to pray. "I'm not taking no for an answer."

Something told me he was telling the truth about that. I decided to agree to go just to get him to let up on me. I could come up with excuses later. "Okay then. I'll have lunch with you."

"Excellent! I'll pick you up here. So when should we go, tomorrow?"

"I don't work tomorrow."

"Then Thursday?"

"Thursday I have something important I need to take care of on my lunch break."

"I'll go with you to run your errand, and then we'll have lunch."

"It's personal."

"Oh, okay." He thought a minute. "Tell you what. I'll drop by again next Tuesday and we'll decide then."

"That's fine."

After Matt left, I entertained the notion of going to lunch with him. Maybe he was right; I was making too much of it. *We're not having an affair; we're going to a public place to eat in the middle of the day.* The more I thought about going to lunch with a handsome, dark foreigner, the more I liked the idea. It sounded so sophisticated and worldly. *We'll do lunch.* I'd never been out to lunch with a man, except for the drive through at the Dairy Maid with Chad. And it was clear Matt was not going to give up. I figured I may as well go and get it over with, just the one time. Chad never even had to know.

The following Tuesday, Matt stopped by the store like he said he would and we agreed to have lunch on Friday. Although I had put up a fight not to go, I found myself looking forward to our date. I liked Matt—as a friend, of course, but he *did* make me feel good about myself.

A COWARD'S DREAM

FRIDAY MORNING, BEFORE my lunch date with Matt, I spent an inordinate amount time trying to decide what to wear. My concern was that I might be too casually dressed. Every time I'd seen Matt he'd had on a suit. The day he came in to confess he'd made up the story about the zippered pants, he'd been wearing a gray suit. When he dropped by to ask me to go to lunch, it was navy blue, and then when he confirmed our lunch date— charcoal pinstripe. With the charcoal suit he'd worn a pink shirt, tie, and matching handkerchief. I remembered thinking I'd never seen a man in pink before. In the world in which I lived, if a man wore pink he was labeled a queer.

After trying on everything in my closet, I chose a soft blue sweater and slimming black pants I'd bought with my first paycheck at Ashley's. The outfit was dressy enough without coming off as trying too hard.

As lunchtime neared, I started to get nervous. I'd told Matt, since I hadn't had a chance to explain to Becky that he was only a friend, to wait outside for me so our leaving together wouldn't raise any suspicion. At twelve o'clock, I went out to the parking lot, and there he was standing beside his car, smiling as usual, not a forced smile, but rather a spontaneous result of being genuinely glad to see me. I couldn't help but smile back. As I'd expected, he had on a suit, a black one with a teal blue shirt and tie. Peeking out of the pocket of his jacket was a silk handkerchief that was a spot on match to his shirt.

As I approached him, he walked around and opened the passenger side door of his car—a sporty red Mazda with black leather seats—and with a welcoming wave of his hand, motioned for me to get in. When we arrived at the restaurant, he got out first and opened the door for me again. By the time we'd walked up to the restaurant entrance and he jumped in front of me to open that door too, I'd figured out I would not be opening any doors while I was with him.

We'd decided to eat at a barbeque place in a neighboring town. I suggested we go there because I thought we would be less likely to run into any of Chad's friends. Not that Matt and I had a reason to hide, but I was married to a man who'd once gotten mad at me for driving to the Kwik Pik to get a Popsicle.

The minute we walked in, everyone in the restaurant turned their eyes to us. Matt was conspicuously different from every other man in town, possibly in western Kentucky. Where we lived he was not considered to be handsome. He was too dark, too foreign, too queer. But by universal standards, except for being on the short side, he was definitely a handsome man. His eyes were deep enough to be sexy, yet soft with compassion. Every jet black hair on his head was in place, unlike the guys I knew that wore shaggy mullets trimmed irregularly by their wives. His light olive skin didn't have a blemish or trace of razor stubble on it. His teeth were all present and straight, and not speckled with chewing tobacco.

Sitting across from him, enjoying his immaculate hygiene, his expensive cologne, I reeked of guilt, because in my mind, I was comparing him to Chad, who always had coal dust in the corners of his eyes and the curves of his ears. Chad, who, no matter how many showers he took, never seemed to get completely clean of the musty smell of the mine.

Despite my nerves leading up to our lunch date, I was surprisingly at ease around Matt. Over soggy pulled pork sandwiches, dill pickle wedges and potato chips, I found out he and his wife, Fatma had come to the United States when they were eighteen to go to college, and had lived here ever since. By the time they graduated, they had both become American citizens.

"So tell me why you're not happy at home?" he asked.

"Chad—my husband—is not a bad man. He's a good father to our kids and a good provider, and he gives me anything I want. But he's so… so… protective. He doesn't want me to go anywhere without him."

"That's not protective; that's controlling," said Matt

"Now he's making me quit my job."

"He's *making* you quit? Tuesday no one has the right

to *make* you do anything. You're married to the man, but he doesn't own you."

He was right; the words sounded absurd even as they came of my mouth, but in the isolation of my small world, it had become accepted behavior.

"You're too beautiful; he's trying to keep you hidden from other men," he said "He's afraid of losing you, but the sad part is by holding on too tight he's pushing you away. The man doesn't want a divorce. He's bluffing."

"Yes I believe you're right. I think he's afraid that if I get out in the world too much he will somehow lose me."

"Go ahead, agree to give him his divorce and see what happens."

"What if he takes me up on the offer?"

"He won't, but if he does, you have to ask yourself if you're willing to continue the rest of your life under his control. Do you love him that much?"

I knew the answer, but I didn't say it out loud.

"If he truly loves you he will want you to be happy, not force you to do something against your will."

"But I'm afraid I couldn't take care of myself without him, let alone my kids."

"You would be surprised what you're capable of. But you'll never know unless you challenge yourself."

"I don't have any family to help me."

"Has your mother passed away too?"

"No, but I can't go to her for help."

"Why?"

"I don't have time to get into that right now."

"So, there's more to the distant sadness in your eyes."

"Yes, much more."

"Tuesday, I want you to know you have a new friend now. I will be there if you need me."

Back at the store, my mind buzzed with all that Matt had said. He'd made me aware of the few remaining threads that sustained my connection to the rest of the world. Under the burden of my fear, I could feel the threads yielding, as though any minute they might break. Would I ever find the courage to enter unknown territory? Or would I take the easy route again, the route on which I knew I would never get lost? If I stayed with Chad, I would slowly withdraw and once again find myself alone inside my head, a dark, scary place to be. And I knew it would be only a matter of time before the emptiness returned. What would fill the void next time? Another obsession? An eating disorder?

By Thanksgiving, I'd made up my mind to leave Chad after Christmas—but I hadn't told him. And I couldn't tell him because if he knew I was thinking of leaving and taking the kids he would do everything in his power to keep me from it. He had once told me if I ever left him he would kill me. I wasn't sure if Chad had it in him to kill, but I knew he was capable of hitting someone in the head with a ball-peen hammer. He grew up in an environment where gun wielding and physical aggression from the alpha male was a tolerated part of the family dynamics. I didn't know how far he would go, because I hadn't pushed him since the night he threatened to shoot Molly and me. I had been a submissive, compliant wife to avoid unleashing the violence inside him, because I was afraid of revisiting the abuse I had escaped. No, I could not tell him I was leaving beforehand. When the time was right I would simply have to leave.

Matt stopped by the store every day on his lunch hour to give me moral support. We went to lunch together once or twice a week.

One day, Becky asked me why he hung around the store much.

"He's just a friend," I said.

"That's not how it appears. The customers are talking, asking about the foreign man who's always in here. It doesn't look good."

"Sorry, Becky; I'll ask him to stay away."

The same afternoon, Matt left work early and came by to see if I was still working. I met him at the door and took him aside. Becky watched my every move from behind the counter.

"Matt, my boss says you're hanging around here too much."

He took offense right away. "Hanging around? This is a public place and I'm a customer."

"But you haven't bought anything."

"Pick something out—anything you want—and I'll buy it," he said, waving his hands around the store. "Then I'll be a customer."

"I can't do that."

"Sure you can. I'm looking for a gift for my dear friend." He pulled a dress from a nearby rack. "This will work." He pulled out another. "And this." He moved to a table of jeans and picked out three pair in size four. "I'll take these as well. I'll need some blouses to go with them—and of course jewelry and purses."

When Matt had finished shopping he had over two hundred dollars worth of clothes and accessories piled on the counter. "Thank you for your help Tuesday," he said, as he filed through a row of one hundred dollar bills in his wallet.

I bagged up his purchase while Becky gave him change for three hundred. As I handed him the bags of clothes, like I did with every other customer, I said, "Thank you for shopping at Ashley's."

He handed the bags back to me. "They're for you." Becky's eyes widened

"Matt, I can't accept all this."

"Consider it an early Christmas present," he said, as he turned to leave the store.

I stuffed the clothes in a cubby under the counter where I kept my purse.

"You need to do something about him before he breaks up your marriage," Becky said.

"We're only friends," I insisted.

"Yeah, right."

I'd been telling myself that Matt and I weren't doing anything wrong because we weren't sleeping together. But on a deeper level, I knew we may as well have been having sex, because the emotional adultery we were committing was as bad, if not worse, than a physical relationship would have been. I enjoyed being with him more than I'd ever enjoyed being with Chad, and he obviously had developed feelings for me. The truth was blatant. We were cheating; we just hadn't consummated our affair—yet.

Christmas was nearing, and I had no solid plan of how to leave Chad. I'd been saving every penny I made at Ashley's, and I still had, in a bank account in Nashville, some college money Daddy had put away for me before he died. There wasn't much left, but enough to put a deposit on a small apartment. Chad still thought I planned to quit my job the day after Christmas, so to buy myself more time to figure out what to do, I told Becky that Chad and I were having problems and needed to be together more so we could talk things out. In light of what she'd observed between Matt and me, she wasn't surprised, and agreed to let me take off work until after the first of the year.

At home, Chad had no idea I was secretly plotting my escape. We had been getting along better since I'd told him I was quitting my job. When his mood was good and he hadn't had too much to drink, I liked Chad. I got a kick out of his cocky bad boy attitude that served to thinly veil his insecurities. And I enjoyed his quick sense of humor. He had an effect on me few people had—he could make me laugh. We got so caught up in the spirit of the holidays, and buying gifts for the kids, I almost forgot how much I wanted to break away from his control.

When I told Matt he was putting my job in jeopardy

by being in the store so much, he stopped coming in. But every day, at lunchtime, he waited for me in the parking lot so we could spend the hour together. We ate in restaurants in one of the neighboring towns, or picked up our food at a drive-thru, and then went to the park and ate in the car with the heater running.

I enjoyed our lunch dates for a while, but things began to get creepy when he started waiting outside the store for me every day when I got off work, just so he could see me for a few minutes before I went home. It seemed like he was always lurking somewhere around me. On my drive home, I often saw the red flash of his car in the rearview mirror, or on the side of the road.

One night, after I got off work, Matt and I were sitting in his car in the store parking lot, and he kissed my hand. "You know by now I want to be with you, Tuesday, but I can't be with another man's woman."

I was attracted to Matt, or maybe awestruck by his mystique, and the attention his dark good looks drew when we walked into a restaurant together. But did I love him? I didn't know. However I *did* know for sure I wasn't leaving Chad to be with him.

"What about you?" I said. "You're still with Fatma."

"Not intimately. We have separate rooms."

"How do I know that?"

"You don't. You'll just have to trust me."

Trust you? The man with the zippered pants? I didn't trust anyone, most of all him.

If leaving his wife would make him happy then I was all for it. I wanted Matt to be happy, but I wasn't sure if I wanted him to be happy with me. I couldn't see how our relationship could grow to be stable when its foundation was built on a lie.

On Christmas morning, Molly and Daryl were wild with glee as they ripped the paper from their presents. Their Christmas couldn't have been any merrier. They got everything they'd asked for, and both Chad and me were giving them our full attention. As far as they knew, Mama and Daddy were doing okay. They had witnessed few fights between us, because I had mastered the skill of compliance to avoid confrontation.

Later that night, they both fell asleep on the sofa, exhausted. I cleared away the wrapping paper, took down the tree and packed it in the attic. Watching Molly and Daryl sleeping, I wondered how I would explain to them why I couldn't live with their daddy anymore. Would they understand if I told them I felt like a prisoner when I was with him? No, they would not, because they couldn't see the bars. My children had once been the center of my life, but now I felt selfish, entitled, like it was my turn. And desperate. Most of all desperate.

Molly and Daryl hadn't asked to be brought into my messy world. Why should they suffer for *my* bad decisions, *my* selfishness, *my* fears, *my* stupid anxiety attacks? How dare I break up our family? Disrupt their comfortable lives? I didn't have the answers to these questions. All I knew was I didn't want to live under Chad's control any longer. And then there was the drinking. I had the occasional glass of wine, but Chad drank half a case of beer every day. The kids had no concept of Chad's problem with alcohol. They had grown up seeing him with a beer in his hand. His drinking had become as routine as their evening baths.

How would I tell them I was inches from filing for a divorce? The reasons weren't good enough. I wasn't miserable enough. And I was a coward. Leaving Chad and living on my own with the kids—independence, freedom, going back to school—was all a dream. A coward's dream.

When it was time for me to return to my job, I waited until after Chad left for the mine, then I got dressed, as usual, and drove to Ashley's. I continued to do this every day I was scheduled to work. I didn't make any extra effort to hide that I was still working, because I didn't care if Chad found out. I didn't have the guts to leave him, but if he put me out on the streets like he'd said he would if I didn't quit working, my problem would be solved.

"I thought I told you to quit that damn job!" he screamed when he found out.

"I won't quit," I said, calmly. "What difference does it make to you anyway as long as I'm home before you and the kids?"

"Fuck it! If it means that much to you to work for pennies, then go ahead, but no more nights or weekends!"

It was just my luck. Like Matt said, Chad had been bluffing all along.

LADYBUG FLY AWAY

A SHLEY'S WAS THE only place for local women to buy halfway stylish clothes of decent quality, so day after day, I saw the same faces come into the store. I thought every woman in the area had shopped there at one time or another, until a slow Monday morning in April when somebody new wandered in, a fresh young face I'd never seen before. She paused at the threshold, holding the door open behind her. She seemed uncomfortable, out of place, as if she'd meant to go into the pharmacy next door, but had inadvertently stumbled into the wrong store by mistake. She was wearing what appeared to be a police uniform—navy blue and mannishly official. Her dark blond hair was cropped and she didn't have on any make-up. I figured her for the type of woman who was so into her career that the way she looked was of low priority. Or she was a lesbian. Either way, I was pretty sure she was in the wrong store.

"Can I help you find something?" I asked.

When she turned her head to look at me, I was startled

by her eyes. They were of a hue and depth blue almost never reaches, like the periwinkles that lined the pathway leading to my Grandma Storm's house—the only safe haven my childhood ever knew.

"No thank you," she said, softly. "Just going to browse, if it's okay."

There was something distinctly familiar about this woman, even though I was positive we had never met. It was more like she reminded me of someone I knew. For the rest of the morning, I racked my brain trying to remember who it was. *She probably resembles a movie star I've seen on TV,* I finally decided.

The next day, the woman with the periwinkle eyes came in again, browsing, but not buying, obviously needing help, but refusing it. She stayed in the store so long, searching through the clearance rack, I thought maybe I should approach her a second time.

"They tell me I'm pretty good at putting together outfits," I said in my most cheerful voice. "I'd love to help you."

"No thank you," she responded, examining the price tag on a sweater. Like a dog that had just been kicked, I scampered away with my tail tucked between my legs.

I had never been one to ponder a customer's behavior, but I couldn't stop thinking about this woman, trying to figure out why she wouldn't let me help her when she was evidently looking for something. She had not been nice to me at all, and she clearly wanted to be left alone, but still, I was drawn to her, which was strange for me because I hardly ever pursued friendship. Other than seeing my volleyball teammates on game nights, I was pretty much a loner.

Friday morning of the same week, she came in the store yet a third time. As always, she headed straight for the clearance rack. Becky and I were behind the counter putting price tags on a new shipment of lingerie. Becky looked up from her work. "Hey Daniela! Never seen *you* in here before. Whatcha looking for?"

"Something on sale," the woman said, as she breezed by the counter.

"We just marked a bunch of stuff down," Becky said. "Tuesday here has great taste; she'll fix you right up."

"You know her?" I whispered to Becky.

"Daniela? Yeah, she's the meter maid. Nice lady."

"Well for some reason she's not nice to *me*."

"She's a bit timid until she gets to know you. Go and show her some of the new markdowns. She'll soften up."

Walking toward Daniela, I felt like a stalker. I was still wincing from her last rejection. "Hello Daniela. Becky asked me to assist you in finding our new markdowns."

To my surprise, she was friendly and chirpy. "I have a date tonight and I don't have a thing in my closet to wear. It's been a while since I've bought any clothes for myself. I'm in the middle of a divorce."

"I knew you were looking for something! Why didn't you let me help you before?"

"Well, I didn't know you for one thing. But now I'm desperate." She laughed

"No worries! I'd be happy to help you."

"I don't have a lot of money to spend."

"Who does? Trust me; we can find something sexy for you to wear on your date right here off this clearance rack."

I'd never had so much fun helping a customer put together an outfit as I did with Dani. Before she left the store, we were both in tears from laughing so hard.

For the rest of the night, I thought about Dani, wondering how her date was going. I couldn't get over how easy it had been to be around her, as though I'd known her all my life. With this on my mind, I floated into a dream.

I am a child—a toddler—strapped in a seat in the back of a moving car. The driver is a woman. I can see only the back of her head, but somehow I know she's my mother. We're going over a bridge. I know this because, through the windows, I can see trusses snap past me. All at once, I hear a deafening crunch, see gray clouds swooshing by. The car begins flipping, flipping and suddenly we hit and water is rising rapidly around us. I begin to cry. The woman—my mother—turns to me. I've never seen her face before, but I recognize her blue eyes—they look like Dani's eyes. As cold water rises up around my neck, she takes my hand in hers. Her touch is warm and loving. "Everything is going to be alright," she says, calmly. "I'll take care of you, I promise." I believe her, even though I know I'm going to die. The water inches up my chin, my lips, and then reaches my nose. I focus on my mother's eyes—soothing, blue eyes, and I'm not afraid.

I woke up sucking air. *What the hell? That was too weird.*

Aunt Macy, a Presbyterian, strongly believed in

reincarnation. In the more than six years I lived with her, we went to church every Sunday, so I was familiar with the meaning of the word, however I was on the fence about whether or not I bought into the concept. I thought coming back to life in another body seemed far-fetched.

Aunt Macy had told me when we meet someone for the first time and feel as though we've known them forever, we probably have known them in a previous life. *Could Dani have been my mother in another life? Had I just dreamt about the way we both died? Is that why, when we first met, I felt like I already knew her?*

The following Monday, Dani stopped in the store to let me know how her date went. The instant I saw her walk in, I lit up. I wanted to run up to her and tell her about my dream, but I knew if I did I would surely run her off, so I kept it to myself.

Over the next couple of weeks, Dani came by whenever she could to chat. Gradually we started opening up to each other about our personal lives. I found out she had twin boys. They were three. She told me her ex-husband had cheated on her with one of her good friends. When she talked about leaving him she sounded relieved.

"The marriage was a shambles long before his infidelity," she said. "He tried to control the way I dressed, who I talked to—everything I did. That's why my hair is short and I don't wear make-up."

There came another night when I wasn't there when

Chad got home from work, and he started in on me again about my job.

"You either quit or I'm filing for a divorce!"

Divorce! It was exactly what I wanted, but hearing the word still intimidated me, because I had no idea how I would properly take care of the kids without Chad, even with child support. I'd foolishly passed up my chance to get an education that would've afforded me a decent paying job. Since Christmas, when I chickened out on leaving him, I'd accepted the idea of living out the rest of my life as his wife, even though I wasn't happy. Happy wasn't the name of the game I was playing. The name of the game was *survival.*

Where will I turn for help if Chad divorces me? Most women turn to family at such a time, but that wasn't an option for me. I didn't have a mother. Jimmy D. had gotten married and moved somewhere in Michigan, and I had no idea where my other brothers were. And the truth was I didn't know any of them well enough to ask for their help anyway. Aunt Macy would take in the kids and me if I asked her to, but I couldn't bring myself to disrupt the cozy life she'd built with Edwin, especially since she'd begged me not to marry Chad in the first place. There was no way out. Chad had me where he wanted me and he knew it.

"Okay, Chad; you win. I'll quit. But let me quit on good terms, in case I have to get another job someday. You've said yourself the mine could go on a long strike when contract time rolls around."

"Whatever; but put in your notice tomorrow."

The next morning, I called Dani and told her about Chad's ultimatum, and confided in her that I wanted to leave him, but felt trapped because I didn't think I could make it on own.

"Sure you can," she said, as if we were talking about baking a cake. "I'll help you."

Her fearlessness excited me. *I can?* "You will?"

"I didn't think I could make it on my own either, but you do what you gotta do. "Don't stay with someone you don't want to be with. It's not fair to you *or* him."

She was right. Chad deserved to be with someone who loved him. The right woman for him was out there somewhere, but as long as he was with me the wrong woman—he would never find her.

"I want to leave, but I'm afraid to even try," I said. "You don't know him, Dani. He will physically restrain me, pull out a gun—whatever it takes to keep me from going."

"Well, I guess we'll have to get you out when he's not there then," she said. "We can do it on your day off while he's at work. I'll help you get your stuff, and you and the kids can stay at my house until you find a place of your own."

I loved her lets-just-do-it way of approaching my problem. For the first time, I believed the freedom I'd dreamt of for so long was possible. With Dani behind me, I had the courage to slay the dragon. And I was ready to try. "Really? You wouldn't mind?" I said.

"Of course not. I know what it's like to be a prisoner in your own home."

The following week, the stars all lined up in my favor. Chad changed to second shift at the mine, opening up the opportunity for me to spend some time with Dani, so we could figure out how and when I was going to leave.

She came over and brought her twins, Bobby Joe, who went by B.J., and Brad. They were bright, adorable boys, and so full of energy and life. Daryl took a liking to them right off, and they looked up to him because he was older, and it didn't take long for Molly to fall in love with Dani.

Later, the kids and I loaded in the car and followed Dani to her house. With Molly's help, I wrote down the exact directions so I wouldn't get lost when I drove there on my own. The following week, while Chad was at work, I took the kids and went to Dani's almost every night so they could get comfortable with her and her house.

One Friday evening when we were at Dani's house, the time felt right. I asked Molly to stay with Daryl and the twins while Dani and I ran an errand. Then we went to the house and got some clothes for the kids and me. While I was there, I left Chad a note to let him know I was gone for good. When Dani and I returned to her house, I told the kids we were staying the night because it was too late to drive home. Daryl was thrilled to sleep over with the twins, and Molly seemed okay with it too.

The next morning after breakfast, when I started getting ready for work, the kids knew something was up. I was in Dani's bathroom putting on my make-up when Molly and Daryl appeared at the door. "When are we going home, Mama?" Molly asked. "Are you taking us before you go to work?"

"No honey. You're going to stay with Dani today while I'm at work. I only work until noon, so it'll only be for a little while."

"Are we going home after you get off work?" she asked.

"I thought we would stay here with Dani again tonight. You guys like Dani, don't you?"

"Yeah, we like her," Molly said. Being the big sister now, she'd taken it upon herself to speak for Daryl too. "But we're ready to go home now."

"We can't go home, Molly. Your daddy and I don't want to live together anymore, and I want you and Daryl with me."

They both glared at me, stunned. I could tell from their faces the news was a complete shock. That was my fault. To them, Mama and Daddy were happy together. Chad *was* happy. His needs were basic. As long as he had his hunting and fishing, his beer and sex, supper on the table by five, life was good. I was the one who had done them a great injustice by faking happiness to make my life easier.

"Did *Daddy* say he didn't want us to live there anymore?" Molly asked.

"No, but he told me he was going to divorce me if I didn't quit my job."

"So quit," she said. "Daddy says you don't have to work anyway."

"But honey, I don't want to quit my job. It's the only

thing I have outside of you and Daryl. And I like having my own money. You understand that, don't you?"

"Daddy will give you money."

"It's not the same."

"So you're leaving Daddy so you don't have to quit your job?"

"No, that's only one reason. There's more; like he doesn't want me to go anywhere without him. But I don't want to get into all that right now."

"Where do you have to go without Daddy?"

"Well, like I said, my job and shopping… and maybe to college someday."

"What did Daddy say when you told him you were leaving?"

"He didn't say anything; he wasn't there. That's where Dani and I went last night, to get some of our clothes."

"Why did you do that?" she asked, angrily. "Now Daddy will think I wanted to leave too and I didn't!" I should have known Molly would rebel. She had always been a daddy's girl.

"I wrote a note. I had to do it that way. You know your daddy; he would have been really ugly if I'd tried to leave while he was there."

She looked at me like it was the end of the world. Regardless of what I told her she wasn't going to understand. To Molly and Daryl there was no reason for us to leave because our life at home was perfect. Daddy paid the bills and Mama cooked and cleaned the house. We went to Grandma's on the weekends. Summertime meant fishing and trips to the sandbar, and of course, the fair. They knew what to expect. They liked the structure. Structure equaled safety.

"Honey, do you remember me telling you that your other grandmother, Mama Rose, was mean to me when I was a little girl?" Molly nodded her head. "Well, it's part of the reason why I need my freedom—I've never really had any. I know this is hard for you to understand, but I feel like a prisoner when I'm with your daddy."

"But Daddy's always been good to you."

She didn't know the whole story, the fights, the drinking, the time he pulled a gun on us, and she didn't need to. "Your daddy is a good provider and he's a good father too. It's just that... you see, your daddy and I have grown to have different goals in life. I want to go to college, and I don't want to spend the rest of my life in Sullivan."

"But I like Sullivan!" Molly's eyes were tearful; her cheeks were bright pink. She was accustomed to getting her way. How could we have kept from spoiling such a darling child? "We're never going back home? When will I see Daddy?"

"You'll see your Daddy on the weekends and whenever you want to."

"Are we going to live here forever?"

"No, this is only temporary until I can find us a place of our own."

"I just want to go home!" she cried. "Why can't we all go home?"

"Honey, I can't take you now, I have to go to work. If you want to go that bad, I'll drive you home this afternoon, but I'll only be dropping you off. I'm coming back here to stay with Dani until I can find us a place to live."

After work, I called Chad and told him I was bringing Molly and Daryl home until I could find an apartment. He was out-of-character calm, which was an unsettling sign.

"I got your note," he said. His voice was hoarse as if he'd spent the previous night yelling. *Or crying?* "It was a hell of a way to break it to me, Tuesday."

"I'm sorry, but we both know what would've happened if I'd tried to leave while you were there."

"Tuesday, quit being stupid and come back home."

"No. I'm not coming home. I won't allow you to control me anymore." Saying the words was empowering and exhilarating—I was reclaiming the independence he'd taken from me. I had been afraid to leave him, and because of that, I had allowed him to dictate my life for ten years. It was my now-look-who-has-no-choice moment.

"What the hell's wrong with you? If the damn job means that much then you can keep it."

"It's too late, Chad. You wanted a divorce and that's what you're getting." It felt good to wad up his threat and throw it back in his face.

"How are you going to pay for an apartment working part-time at Ashley's? You can't make it on your own," he said. "You'll be back."

"No, Chad, you're wrong. Even if I have to live on the streets, I'm never coming back."

GOING BACK

THE FOLLOWING MONDAY, I filed the divorce papers and found an apartment. I thought it would be a good idea to put some distance between Chad and me, so I rented a place in Uniontown that had once been a motel before the rooms were remodeled into studio apartments. It had a furnished living room/kitchen combo and one tiny bedroom—a giant leap down from the house we were accustomed to. But it was all I could afford and a quick fix for the kids.

Molly hated the apartment the minute she walked in. The whole place was barely bigger than her room at home. "Where will I sleep," she asked, looking around.

"It looks like we're all going to have to sleep in the same room for a while. It'll be fun!"

"Where's the kitchen?"

"Over there." I pointed across the dingy living room to a wall with a sink, a two burner stove and a waist high refrigerator. "Isn't it cozy?"

She scowled and stomped over to the ragged sofa and plopped down.

Daryl, on the other hand, made a quick transition. He befriended a black boy around his age who lived next door, and they spent their days shooting basketball in a goal someone had erected in front of the complex. Daryl didn't have much to say about the separation. Molly did all the talking for the two of them. He, like his daddy, had never been a big talker, but now he was even quieter than usual. This concerned me. I wished he would lash out, like Molly, instead of keeping it all in.

Not long after we moved into the apartment, Dani and I needed some relief from the stress of our impending divorces. We were ready for our first girl's night out as free women. We scraped together a few dollars and offered to pay Molly if she would watch Daryl and the twins while we went out. She wasn't happy about the idea, but reluctantly agreed.

There was nowhere for us to go in Uniontown, so we decided to try a dance club we'd heard about in Henderson, a few miles away. We curled and teased our hair, making it as big as we could, lined our eyes inside and out, put on the best dresses we owned, and headed out to party. Neither one of us had ever been to a dance club before.

The club was packed and the energy inside was intoxicating. Rhythmic music blared out over clean-cut men in plaid oxford shirts, and pretty, young women wearing revealing tops and skin-tight jeans. We weren't sure what to do when we walked in. Dani didn't drink, and neither of us had any money, so we stood by the door and watched everybody else have fun.

Before too long, we were both asked to dance. I didn't know about Dani, but I'd never danced before, except in the privacy of my home. When we got out on the floor, we figured out there was no structure—everyone created their own freeform movements. When we realized how easy it was, we both came alive with the music, and discovered something new about ourselves—we loved to dance. We couldn't get enough. If nobody asked us, we danced with each other.

Everything was going great. Men were buying me drinks, and there was no shortage of interesting people to talk to. Then I spotted Chad at the bar staring at me and everything went to hell. *Did he troll the bars and dance clubs until he found me? Or is he just trying to move on with his life too? After all, it is the only decent place to go within twenty miles.*

Chad made his way across the dance floor through the sweaty, swaying bodies to where I was standing. "I found out why you're *really* leaving me," he said, blankly. After ten years of marriage, I thought I knew Chad well, but this time I couldn't read what he was thinking from his expressionless face. *Is he hurt? Is he furious? What is his next move?* "A camel jockey," he yelled, his voice resounding through the music. "You're leaving me for a fuckin' camel jockey!"

"Chad, let's talk about this somewhere else." I walked toward the door, and he followed. Dani came off the dance floor and joined us.

"A fuckin towelhead!" he screamed as soon as we got outside. "All that shit about control and independence was a lie!"

"No it wasn't! Yes, I've been seeing someone as a friend, but I'm not leaving you to be with him."

"You've been *seeing* someone? You mean you've been *fucking* someone!"

"No I haven't! We started out as friends."

"You expect me to buy that load of crap?"

"It makes no difference to me what you think anymore. I don't want to be with you."

"I can't believe your breaking up our family for a camel jockey! How can you do this to our kids?" He shoved me. "You slut!"

Dani came over and got between Chad and me. "Who in the fuck are you?" he said, pushing her to the ground.

When I saw Dani on the blacktop in her new blue dress, I remembered why I was divorcing Chad. "Leave us alone!" I told him. "Or I'll have a bouncer throw your scrawny ass in the street!"

I helped Dani up. "Did he hurt you?" I asked.

"Nah, I'm tough," she said. "Maybe it's time for us to leave though." I nodded my head in agreement. We hurried to Dani's car and pulled out of the parking lot.

"You're right;" Dani said. "He's mean, and he's an asshole too!"

"Dani, I'm so sorry."

"Don't be. It's not your fault you married an asshole. I married one too."

We both laughed.

211

"Who the hell is the camel jockey?"

I hadn't told her about Matt. There had been so much going on with us, I honestly hadn't thought of it. "His name's Matt and he's someone I've been seeing every now and then."

"Why did Chad call him a camel jockey?"

"He's from the middle east. You know how rednecks are."

"Wait a minute; I know this guy. He's a good looking dark-haired man, right? I think his last name is *Demir*, or something like that?"

"Yes. How do you know him?"

"Sometimes while I'm working, I stop in businesses and visit with people I know." She crinkled her nose. "I'm not sure about this guy, Tuesday. I've seen him everywhere, and I know a lot of women he's come onto. I think he's a player."

This news did not surprise me or upset me in the least. My indifference helped me to better understand how Matt fit into my life. "Really? Thanks for the head's up."

As time went by, it got harder and harder to get Molly to come back with me when I picked her up from Chad's. And then the whole time she was with me she complained about missing her bed, her stuff, and the big screen TV.

"I want to live at home with Daddy," she said, after less than a month in the motel apartment.

I knew Chad would never go for the kids living with

him, so I wasn't too worried about what she was saying coming to fruition, but I was still hurt that she'd even said it. My heart was crying, but on the outside you would never have known. As a child, I'd learned to turn my emotions off during Mama's belittlement and torture games, so she wouldn't know she was hurting me, because when she found something she knew caused me pain she always did it more. This protective mechanism had worked for me then, but as an adult, made me sometimes come off as cold and insensitive. "Did you tell your Daddy about this?"

"Yep, and he said it's okay."

He's probably bluffing again to try to get me to come back home. "Is that so? What will you do while he's at work?"

"The same thing I do while you're at work. Only when we're with Daddy, sometimes we stay with Grandma or Aunt Lilly."

"Who will cook for you?"

"Daddy can make hamburgers and spaghetti. Grandma cooks for us most of the time anyway."

Damn it Bobbi. I should have known you'd step in. How could I compete with Chad's family support? I had no one to help me, except Dani, and she had her hands full as it was. "How nice of Grandma," I said.

"Daddy needs me. He's sad by himself." Molly said, boldly. "You're not even sad without him. You have Dani and you go out and dance."

The relief from being out from under Chad's watch must have shown. "Your daddy has his family. They can keep him company."

"He says it's not the same as us."

"Well I need you too Molly!"

"Not as much as Daddy. He said you have a boy-friend. Daddy called him a towel head. We hate towel heads."

"I don't have a boyfriend... not like your daddy thinks... and the man he's talking about is just a friend."

"Daddy said you want a divorce so you can be with your boyfriend."

"That's not true!"

Right there I stopped, stepped back and took inventory of the situation. To Molly, I was the bad guy—the one who had ruined everything. In her eyes, Chad was the victim, the underdog. He had made it clear he wanted me to come back home and that he didn't want a divorce, which left me scrambling for reasons for single-handedly breaking up our family. The reasons I gave felt valid in my heart, but came out of my mouth sounding selfish and trivial.

I looked over at Daryl, who was watching TV. "What about you, honey. What do you want to do?"

"I don't care," he said in a disinterested tone. "I don't want to go to school here, though. All my friends are in Sullivan."

"Sullivan's not far away; I can drive you and pick you up in the afternoons."

He turned to his sister. "What are *you* gonna do, Molly?"

"I'm living with Dad. He needs me. He doesn't have a girlfriend," she said, cutting her eyes at me.

"I told you I don't have a boyfriend!" *Do I?*

Daryl looked away from the TV. "Mama, if I live with you and Molly doesn't, who will stay with me while you're at work?" he asked.

I hadn't even thought of that. To help me out financially, Becky had increased my hours, so I'd started working nights and weekends—anytime I could. Dani had her mother to keep her twins. I didn't have a mother. I didn't have anyone. And I couldn't afford a sitter every day.

"I don't know right now; I'll have to come up with something."

"I better live with Dad then," said Daryl. "Grandma will let me stay with her." He turned back to the TV.

This wasn't supposed to happen. The mother always gets the kids. I reminded myself that Chad would not want Molly and Daryl to live with him once he realizes he can't use them to blackmail me into coming back home. "Your dad is not totally innocent in all this, you know."

"I know," Molly said. "He told me he did some things wrong, but he's sorry, and now he's trying to get you back. You won't even try to get back together. You could at least try!"

Daryl got up from watching TV. "Yeah, Mom; you could at least try."

Maybe I owe them the effort to try to work things out with their daddy. Maybe I owe it to Chad.

Chad had grown up in an atmosphere where family always came first and stayed together at all cost. I was raised the same way. Sort of. Countless times I watched Mama beat Daddy in the face with the backs of both her fists, and he took her punches without putting his hands on her. Watching this, I'd wondered why he didn't leave her. He saw her beat me in the same way. But did he desert her even then? No. Because he didn't want to break up the *family*.

"Yes, you're right; I *could* give it a try, and I'll think about it, but only if you'll try to live in this apartment for a while first."

They both cheerfully agreed.

For the next several days, the pros and cons of a reconciliation with Chad was all I thought about. If I went back to him, at least I would have my kids with me all the time and they would be happy because they would be living in the house they loved with their parents together. And I'd be certain to survive—have a roof over my head, food to eat. Survival was the name of the game—the only game I knew how to play. Sure, I would spend my days languishing in depression, turn myself inward again and crawl back inside the dark recesses of isolation. But no one would know of my misery, because I would keep my emotions pent up to avoid an argument. My eating disorder would probably come out of hiding. No, it definitely would come out. But the kids would be happy. The kids would be happy. The kids would be happy, and I would be okay somehow, because I was a cockroach.

One weekend when I dropped the kids off with Chad, he came outside and stood on the front porch. His face looked like it had been run through a meat grinder. "What the hell happened to you?" I asked.

"Bar fight."

"Over what?"

"I had too much to drink and started running my mouth. Guess I was taking my anger out on the wrong person."

Molly burst into tears. She ran to him and wrapped her arms around his waist. Daryl joined her. "Daddy, are you okay? I missed you!" Molly cried.

Chad looked so pitiful standing on the front porch of the house we had built together, his face almost unrecognizable, our children clinging to him. It took everything I had to resist the impulse to run up and hug him too.

School started, and like I'd promised, every morning I drove Molly to Junior High and Daryl to elementary in Sullivan. And like Molly had promised, she tolerated the motel apartment, but not a single day passed that she didn't remind me how much she hated living there. Several times a week, both she and Daryl asked me when I was going to "at least try" to work things out with Chad. I gave in, and agreed to go back in two and a half weeks when the current month's lease was up on the apartment.

The closer it got to the end of the month, the more I began to regret having told the kids I would try to reconcile with Chad. Right when I'd made the decision to back out of the agreement, something changed my mind. I was going through some of Daryl's school papers and ran across one where he had listed some of the things for which he was thankful. Number one on the list: *I am thankful that my mama and daddy are getting back together soon.* Alone, clutching that paper, I read it over and over and wept for hours. *How could I let Daryl down?*

Matt called me at work the next day and asked if I would meet him for lunch. Our meetings were less clandestine now that I was legally separated from Chad. The town was well aware that there was something going on between the two of us. The rumors were much more scandalous and exciting than the reality. The adulteress and the—gasp—towel head!

I enjoyed Matt's company. He opened doors for me and bought me nice gifts. When I was around him, he almost made me believe I was pretty. I liked how he dressed and smelled, and the way his words softly rolled off his tongue. But I did not want to be in a permanent relationship with him. There were too many things I *didn't* like about him. I didn't like the creepy way he seemed to be everywhere I was. And I didn't trust him. Our relationship was based on a lie about zippered pants. He wanted me to leave Chad because he was afraid of the drunken coal miner with guns, but he had no intention of leaving his wife. Money was involved, and a sick child. Much easier to keep the wife and take a naïve mistress. He was an intelligent man and he sensed the vulnerability in me—an easy target. And now I'd found out he was a player. Because of all this, I knew we weren't going to be together long term. I just hadn't figured out how I was going to break away from him.

We ate at one of the few restaurants in town. As always, everyone in the place stared at us when we came in, as if we were actors walking onto a stage. Matt pulled out a wobbly wooden chair for me. I sat, picked up the paper napkin from the table, unfolded and placed it in my lap. As soon as we had put in our drink order, I said, "I told the kids I would try to work things out with Chad."

"What? Are you insane? You were lucky to get away from him. Do you think he will ever allow you to leave again?"

"I feel like I should do it for the kids. I've tried, but can't make them understand why I'm leaving. The reasons I give them all seem... *selfish*."

"Of course they're selfish! You have to look out for yourself. Believe me Tuesday, when your children are grown and the time comes for them to make the decision whether or not they should leave you and pursue their own lives, they won't think twice. And they shouldn't, because they have the right to seek happiness the same as you do."

"Well, you're one to talk, Matt," I said. "By the way, how are your divorce proceedings coming along?"

"I told you I would have to work into that slowly..."

"Whatever."

"What difference does it make if you're going back to Chad?" Although I'd pointed out otherwise on more than one occasion, he still thought I was leaving my husband for him.

Dani was supportive when I called and told her of my decision to try to make my marriage work. "If you don't try you'll always wonder. And if it doesn't work out, at least you'll know you did everything you could."

I needed to hear that.

When the lease was up on the apartment, I got my things together and moved back in with Chad. The instant I entered the house, I was thirteen-years-old again, locked in an attic.

Chad was on his best behavior for a couple of days. Then he suggested I quit my job again. That was enough for me to realize he hadn't changed.

I managed to somehow stay a week before I called Dani. "I can't do it, I said, shaking so much I could barely hold the phone. "If I stay any longer I'm afraid I'll have a breakdown."

"At least you tried, sweetie," she said.

"The kids are going to hate me; they're so happy now because they think Chad and I are together for good. I'm afraid I may have made it worse by coming back. Now they have their hopes up."

"What good would you be to them, or Chad, if you had a breakdown? Look, you stayed with him and put up with that godforsaken family of his longer than you should have for the kids, right? Do something just for yourself for once. I know you don't think you deserve it, but you do. The kids will adjust."

"Dani, how do you always know the right thing to say?"

"Get your stuff together. You're coming to stay with me while you look for another apartment."

THE HIGH PRICE OF PANTYHOSE

MOLLY AND DARYL were with Chad, and Dani's twins were at their dad's for the weekend. I called Dani from work. "We need a girl's night out. It will give you a chance to wear the new red dress we picked out for you."

"Sounds great, but I'll have to stop and get some pantyhose if I'm wearing a dress."

"Good because I need some too."

"We'll stop at the Bigfoot in Henderson and pick some up. I've got to get gas anyway."

When Dani and I walked into the Bigfoot, we drew plenty of attention from the men in the store. Not many women wore dresses where we lived, and back then, nobody went bare-legged. We selected our pantyhose—sheer black, because our pumps were black—paid for them, and the gas, and then headed back out to the car to put our new hose on.

Putting panty hose on in the car was not new to us. It seemed like we were always running them when we went out. We'd actually gotten pretty good at the technique. We let our seats all the way back so we could stretch our legs out, and then we began to wiggle into our hose. In no time, I had mine on, but it was taking Dani longer because she had the steering wheel to contend with.

"Uh-oh," she said, when she had the hose halfway up her second leg.

"What?"

"I just put my fingernail through mine."

I laughed. "Run back in the store and get another pair."

"I can't go back in there. I just *bought* pantyhose. They'll think I'm nuts."

"Well, I can't go in either then."

"Let's drive up the road to the Sureway. I'll get some there."

Dani bought another pair of panty hose at the grocery store and put them on without incident. She started the car engine, and I leaned back in my seat to get comfortable for the ride. Finally we were all set to go dancing.

As we pulled out of the parking lot, I crossed my legs and the bottom of the glove box caught my new hose ever so slightly. I was afraid to look. *Please don't let there be a run.*

"Dani, you're not going to believe this," I said.

"Don't tell me you ran your hose."

"Bad. I need another pair."

She turned the car around. I went in the Sureway for my second pair of hose, and then put them on in the car.

"This time I won't cross my legs," I assured Dani.

"It's probably best."

After all that, we needed a cigarette. We smoked only when we went out, and even then, we didn't inhale all the way. Smoking gave us something to do with our nervous hands.

In turn, Dani and I each lit our cigarettes with the car lighter. As I was putting the lighter back, a tiny spark of lit tobacco spat out and landed on my leg. I slapped at the spark until, thankfully, I was able to extinguish it. The bad news? The spark burned a huge hole in my second pair of pantyhose.

Dani and I glared at the ring of exposed flesh on my leg, now red from all my slapping. We both busted out laughing, and laughed until we'd ruined our mascara and had to reapply it.

When she caught her breath, Dani said, "There's another Bigfoot up the road."

"It's your turn," I joked, as we were walking up to the Bigfoot. She decided to buy a spare pair of hose, just in case.

Coming out of the store, we were still laughing intermittently, having more fun than we would have had at any bar or nightclub, when, suddenly, I saw something that made me stop laughing and freeze in my tracks.

"What's wrong, sweetie?" Dani asked.

"There's my mother."

"Where?"

"Over there by the gas pumps," I said, as if I'd spotted a vicious wild animal. "Oh my God, she's looking this way." Aware of how my reaction might have seemed to Dani, who knew nothing of my childhood, I added, "I'm shocked to see her here, that's all. She lives in Tennessee."

Dani pulled my arm. "Well, come on, let's go say hi! I can't wait to meet her!"

Mama began walking toward us. "Hey there, Ladybug," she said. "How ya been?"

"Mama, what are you doing here?"

"I'm getting gas. I'm on my way to Michigan to see your brother."

Unbelievable, I thought. *What are the chances of Mama and me both being at the same Bigfoot at exactly the same time? Fate is a cruel bitch.* "Is that so," I said.

"Where are you girls headed?" Mama asked, casually.

"We're going to a dance club."

"Really? I miss my dancing days. You'd better enjoy it while you're young!"

Dani nudged me. "I'm sorry. Dani, this is my mother, Rose."

"It's so nice to finally meet my best friend's mother!"

"Nice to meet you too, Dani. Is Dani short for Danielle?"

"Daniela."

"Beautiful name."

"Speaking of beauty, isn't my Ladybug the most beautiful girl you've ever laid eyes on?"

"Mama, *please.*"

"Well, you are! You're gorgeous! Isn't she Daniela?"

"You probably need to be getting back on the road," I said. "You've got a long way to go."

"I was thinking of staying in Henderson for the night."

"Oh no," I said. "You would hate the motels in Henderson. I've heard some of them are roach-infested." Dani gave me an strange look.

"Well I guess I'll get a room in the next town then. You know how much I hate cockroaches!"

The three of us stood there in uncomfortable silence for a few long seconds. Mama finally spoke up. "Well, I'd better get going."

"Yeah, us too," I said. "Bye." I pulled Dani's arm in the direction of the car.

Dani turned to Mama as we walked away. "Nice to meet you, Rose!"

"I'll call you, Ladybug!" Mama hollered out.

Yeah, right, I thought. *You don't even have my number, and I intend to keep it that way.*

As soon as we were in the car, Dani asked, "What's the deal with your mother?"

"It depends on what you mean."

"Well, first off, where were the hugs? You haven't seen each other in *forever* and neither of you made a move to give the other a hug."

"We're not huggers."

"And she didn't even ask about your kids. Then—no offense, Tuesday—there was all the gushing about how beautiful you are. You *are* a pretty girl, but I'm sorry it sounds so... so... *fake*. It's just not how a normal mother acts."

Although the trust I had for Dani had been instantaneous, and was now complete, I still hadn't found the courage to talk to her about my past. When people found out, their attitude toward me changed. I couldn't risk Dani thinking I was a liar, or—if she believed me—a freak. And I couldn't bear the thought of her looking at me in the piteous way people did after I told them. Dani and I had something special—something pure—and I wanted to keep our friendship unmarred by my lurid past for as long as I could. Now I had no choice but to tell her. If I didn't it would be the same as lying. I took a deep breath. "My mother hates me."

"I believe it," she said.

"What? *Really?*" I had said the exact words to others before her, only to be met with disbelief and debate. No one had ever said they believed me without hesitation, without a doubt.

"Oh, yeah; I wasn't going to tell you this, but as we were walking away and I turned to wave at her, the look she gave you behind your back was pure hate."

Dani and I never made it to the dance club that night. We'd already spent too much time running panty hose, and I was out of the mood anyway. We went to her place, and over several cups of coffee, I told her everything. Not the generalized story most people got, but every sordid detail I could remember. The words flowed, and with them came all the emotions I'd been holding back for so long.

With sincere concern, and genuine tears pooling in her eyes, Dani gave me her full attention, sitting quietly until I got it all out. Her total faith that what I was saying was true breathed life into my story. *It did happen.* Talking openly and honestly helped me to understand that the most significant hindrance to my healing process had been my inability to discuss the details of my childhood abuse. Telling Dani was a positive step, possibly my first on the path to healing.

TUESDAY'S ECLIPSE

A S THE DIVORCE proceedings progressed, things began to go south quickly. Chad's mine shut down, putting him out of work indefinitely. He called and told me he couldn't continue to pay child support. "You can't get blood from a turnip," were his exact words. But he assured me he would provide for Molly and Daryl. When I asked him how he proposed to do that without a job, he said, with his family's help, he could pay the house payment and take care of the kids, but only if they lived with him. Bobbi had told him she wouldn't give him a dime to pay me, but would gladly help take care of Molly and Daryl.

When I hung up the phone from talking to him, I immediately dialed the lawyer representing both of us. As soon as I got her on the line and told her my name, I started in. "Chad says he's going to stop paying child support!"

"He tells me he's been laid off from work," she said. "If he has no income, he can't continue to pay the current amount of support. We'll have to adjust his payment amount, and I can tell you the reduction will be significant. He told me he can't promise he can even pay the reduced amount."

"But the court will make him pay, right?"

"Yes, eventually. But things could get rough for you and the kids in the meantime."

"I know he could get the money from his family," I said.

"Maybe so, but we can't make him. If he doesn't pay anything, you can have him put in jail for contempt of court. But do you really want to do that?"

"I can't. The kids already blame me enough as it is."

"Will your family give you money for the mortgage payment so you can stay in the house with the kids?"

"Don't have any family."

"Oh."

"No, and I don't want the house anyway. His family lives all around there and they aren't fond of me."

"You could sell it, but Chad told me you've also taken out a second mortgage. So selling is probably not a good option for you, because if the house goes for less than you owe the bank, since the mortgage is in both your names, you'll be responsible for your half of the difference."

"Chad can keep the house."

"The court will most likely award you physical custody and order a child support payment. But Chad said it could be a while before he goes back to work. Do you have the means to provide for your children in case he's stubborn about paying support?"

"No, I can barely make it with the money he's been paying."

"Divorce is never good for children, but sometimes it's unavoidable. You and Chad have to ask yourselves what's best for Molly and Daryl. What would be the smoothest transition for them?"

"To stay in the house, but that's not happening because I can't afford the payment."

"Look, Chad has agreed to keep Molly and Daryl in the home they are accustomed to. With his family's help, he says he can pay the house payment and make sure the children are provided for. He tells me it's where they want to live anyway."

"They only want to live there because it's more comfortable for them. I can't tell you how many times I've had the *big screen TV* thrown in my face."

She chuckled. "Naturally they're going to want to stay where the best stuff is. Kids don't like change, but they adjust. Like I told Chad, my suggestion is to do what's best for the children."

"But I'm not giving up my kids."

"You won't be. They'll just be living with Chad and continuing school and other activities as usual. Your custody will be fifty-fifty. You'll see them on the weekends, and of course, there will be more time for them to stay with you during the holidays and in the summer. Chad seems to be very agreeable in this area."

"But his family will be taking care of the kids most of the time. He's only doing this because he doesn't want to pay child support."

"Well, no man wants to pay child support. But in Chad's case, I believe he honestly *can't* pay it. Look at it this way. At least he's willing to take the kids. Most men aren't. It would be much harder on you if you had to try to find a means to support your children on your own. I can try to get you a small support payment to help out when the children are living with you."

I hung up the phone and dropped my head into my hands. *What do I do now? Do I force Molly and Daryl to live with me against their will? Or do what's best for them and let them live with Chad in the house they love surrounded by family?*

It didn't take me long to make up my mind. I decided to force them to live with me. It's a mother's natural instinct to want her kids with her, to *expect* them to be with her, whether she can support them or not. Usually the father doesn't want them because he doesn't think he can care for them. But this father has help. Lots of help. *It doesn't matter; it's a given; the mother gets kids, the father pays support. Done deal.*

Not long after I'd made my decision, the situation got even worse. Chad called to tell me that Molly—from out of nowhere—announced she would testify in court that I was an unfit mother if I didn't let her live in the house with her dad.

"I don't know why she said it," he said, his words tinged with sarcasm. "I think it's got something to do with the camel jockey you've been seeing."

"I don't believe you!"

"You can ask her yourself."

"I will!" I slammed the phone down.

I dialed Dani's number. "Dani, something terrible has happened! Chad just told me if I don't let the kids live with him Molly said she's going to testify in court that I'm an unfit mother!"

"That bastard!"

"Do you think she actually said it?"

"Honestly? With the way she's been acting whenever she's at your apartment—like she's miserable—yes. Sweetie she's only a kid. Chad probably told her you would come back home if she said that. Or the lawyer said it was the only way he could get custody of the kids and not have to pay child support, and he told Molly it was the only way she could live with him. You know Chad and the Suttons put the idea in her head and the words in her mouth. How else would Molly even know what an unfit mother is? It's not something that normally comes out of the mouth of a twelve-year-old."

"I've never abused my kids! Maybe I haven't given them the attention I should have, especially lately..."

"Stop it, Tuesday! You are not an *unfit mother*. Just because you have to work a lot, and don't have a family to help you, and you can't afford a nice place to live and a big screen TV, doesn't mean you're not a good mother. And because you go out to dance once in a while, maybe have a laugh or two, doesn't mean you don't love your kids. Chad goes out—does that make him an unfit father? No. Just because you put yourself first for once in your life, and claim some happiness you rightly deserve doesn't make you a bad person, or a bad mother."

"Thanks Dani; you always know what to say to make me feel better."

"I'm not saying it to make you feel better; it's true."

"I just thought of something else. Chad's family would probably testify against me too. They would do anything to help Chad get custody. What if they reveal that I was a victim of child abuse? You know what they say about abuse victims."

"I don't care. It's simply nonsense and it won't hold up in court, even if Molly does testify. They'd have to prove it and they can't. I'll testify if I have to."

"I know you would."

"But to be honest with you, sweetie, you *are* in a bad position. You don't have family to watch the kids while you work, or help you out financially, and Chad does. I wish I could help, but I'm hanging on by a thread myself. If I didn't have my own family I don't know how I would make it."

"Dani, what am I going to do?"

"The way I see it you have three choices. None of them are pleasant, and two are probably out of the question. Do you want to hear them?"

"I think I already know, but yeah, go ahead."

"You can, one, force the kids to live with you. Two, let them live in the house with Chad. Or three, you can go back. But don't do the last one. You've already tried that once and it sent you into hysterics."

"I'll force the kids to live with me."

"I don't blame you. But if you do, you run the risk of Molly saying you're an unfit mother, just so she can live with Chad and the big screen TV. Even though it would never hold up in court, to hear her say it would crush you even though we both know she doesn't mean it. It would be your worst fear coming true. And if Chad doesn't pay support, how will you afford to buy the kids' clothes and school supplies on your own? What about court costs and lawyer fees? The bills will pile up fast if this goes to court."

"I'll keep Daryl then. I know he will stay with me."

"You can't afford a sitter for when you work nights and weekends. And what about summer?"

She was right—about all of it. Staying with me wasn't what was best for Molly and Daryl. It was best for me. Because I didn't have money or family, unless I caved in to Chad and went back, I had only one choice. "I have to let them live with him."

"It's not like you're losing them."

"At least I'll know Chad's family will see to it they're taken care of."

"Tuesday, whatever you decide to do you need to try to be happy for once in your life—if for no other reason than to see what it's like."

After almost a year of dragging our feet, Chad and I finalized our divorce. He kept the house, and so the kids' lives wouldn't be disrupted, we agreed their primary residence would be there with him, for the time being. I would get them on weekends and in the summer.

The day I signed those papers agreeing to let Molly and Daryl live away from me was when the descent began. As soon as I put down the pen, I began sinking back into the black abyss I'd known as a child, and this time I knew pulling myself out wouldn't be easy. I wanted to curl up in a ball on the floor, but instead, I did what any true survivor would have done in my situation—I shut off my emotions so I could get up, put one foot in front of the other and go on functioning. Like I had done so many times as a child, I became numb.

Dani had said it would crush me to hear Molly say I was an unfit mother, but even though I hadn't heard the words come out of her mouth, I still I felt like I'd been run over by a tank. Ironic how the one person who had turned my emotions on was responsible for turning them back off again. But I tried not to blame Molly, and kept telling myself Chad and his family were behind it all. I never confronted her about her decision to live with Chad—I couldn't bring myself to even talk about it. I'd become the coward my daddy once was, inherited his most despicable trait—the ability to turn away from problems and pretend they didn't exist.

I was used to having my children close by every day, knowing they were safe, hearing their laughter. I missed Molly's sleepy eyes at bedtime. Tripping over Daryl's toy cars scattered around the floor. I was afraid I had made the biggest mistake of my life.

Chad and I divided up our belongings amicably.

Because the kids were with him, I agreed to let him keep most of the furniture and all the appliances. I settled for 100 dollars a month child support for when the kids were with me, but Chad didn't even pay that. He could no longer afford the payment on my car—a used Firebird we'd bought a few years earlier—and neither could I, so we sold it, paid off the loan, and split the remaining money. With my part, I bought an old beater to get me to work and pick up the kids, a rusty Chevy Chevette with a rickety engine and a black smoke shadow.

Chad recovered and was doing fine. Better than fine. He was happier than I'd ever seen him. He'd been seeing someone he had met not long after our separation, and she had already moved in with him. Into our house. The house we built together. She was a pretty hairdresser who ran her own business. The kids liked her. She had great hair. Chad was obviously crazy about her. I could tell by the way his mouth turned up at one corner when he said her name, like he was trying to be cool and suppress a smile, but his joy was so overwhelming he couldn't. I'd seen him smile that way only once before.

I was happy for Chad, happy he'd found someone. Truly I was. He was the kind of man who needed a woman in his life, and knowing he had companionship helped to ease the guilt I still carried for leaving him. But I was jealous. Not of his new woman, or even them being together, but of his tolerance of her independence. From talking to the kids, I'd learned she spent most of her time at her beauty shop. Why was it okay for her to be away from him so much? Had there been something about *me* that made Chad possessive and controlling?

The divorce papers had been signed. Molly and Daryl were content with the custody arrangement. Chad had found his soul mate. And I was lost, as usual. Freedom was not what I had expected. Being on my own reminded me of when I was a kid, and had finally succeeded in picking the lock on my bedroom door so I could steal some food from the kitchen. For so long, I had wanted nothing more than to be out of that locked room, but the instant I stepped into the world of the free—the world in which the rest of my family lived—I was overcome with fright. There was too much space outside my tiny room, too many choices. As depressing as it was to be locked up every day, somehow the boundaries of my confinement had made me feel safe. There were no more boundaries for me now. No getting my old life back. No more chance for a sure thing. Every day that lay ahead of me was a big fat scary mystery. But that's what I'd signed up for, what I *had* to have.

Without Molly and Daryl by my side, I was miserable, except on the nights Dani and I went out. On those nights, I wore tight dresses and puffed on cheap cigarettes while I mingled with strange men, pretending the drinks they bought me were for reasons other than to try to take me to bed. In the low light of a smoky bar, I was *almost* pretty and the drunken men that came on to me found me to be *almost* desirable. Out on the dance floor, with a decent buzz, was the only time I could clear my head of Mama's belittling words, Chad's possessive control, and the fear—there was so much fear. I danced for every party I never went to, every date I never had, and for a few hours, I was happy—superficial, tequila-soaked happy. Happy, until the next morning when my head was cleared of alcohol, and the sunlight found my mascara-streaked face and I remembered my children were not there. That's when I pulled the covers over my head in shame for daring to have fun without them.

Matt remained a distant, blurry figure in the ever changing landscape of my life. He filed for a divorce from his wife, Fatma, and showed me a copy of the papers he had yet to finalize. For the sake of their sick son, and perhaps convenience, they agreed to continue living together in the same house after their divorce, but they would sleep in separate rooms. Or so he said. I didn't pressure him to leave Fatma, because I didn't want him to. She was my safety net. Her presence prevented him from trying to force a commitment from me. Matt was always there, somewhere nearby, looming in the parking lot at Ashley's, or waiting for me at a secluded table in a dimly-lit restaurant. I met him discretely once or twice a week, and we drove to a neighboring town for drinks or dinner. Sometimes we got a room in an out of the way motel. He was always there, but he was never really *with* me.

Neither Matt, nor Chad, nor any other man was equipped with the tools needed to knock down the stout wall I'd erected between me and the rest of the world. Matt kept insisting we would be married someday, and I listened as he made plans for us, knowing all the while we would never be together in that way. Being the coward I was, I didn't tell him otherwise, or put a stop to whatever we had. I wasn't quite sure how to break off a relationship that had begun with a lie, and therefore, in my mind was not legitimate. So I kept seeing him, waiting for something to happen to make it go all away.

Matt's wife somehow found out about me. One night, as I was closing up at work, I spotted her looming outside the door. Draped in a black hooded cape, she stood staring dead at me like the Grim Reaper waiting for a chance to take me out. Even though I'd never laid eyes on Fatma before, I knew the shadowy figure I saw was her. She was the only darkly exotic, forty-something woman that would've had an interest in me. Later, when I told Matt, he confirmed it had been her outside the store, and said she was just curious to see what I looked like. I said she was nuts.

Ashley's went out of business and I was temporarily unemployed, until a friend got me a job at the local newspaper selling ads. Every now and then, they let me write a feature story. The writing I enjoyed, but I wasn't good at the selling part, because I got lost all the time while servicing the ads. The job didn't pay much, so I started looking for something else right away.

Jobs were scarce in the area, unless you wanted to work in the coal mines, or the pants factory, or Job Corps, the delinquent youth rehabilitation center where my daddy had worked. Retail was all I knew. There were a few mom and pop stores, but most of those positions were filled by relatives of the owners. It took a while, but I found work at a furniture store owned by one of my newspaper advertisers. The pay was better—a small base hourly wage plus commission—but the evenings I sometimes had to work were challenging when the kids were with me.

FLICKERS IN THE DARK

D ANI LANDED A great job as an administrative
assistant at a product research company in
Evansville, Indiana, right across the Ohio River from
Henderson. She quickly made plans to move away from
Uniontown and get an apartment in either Henderson or
Evansville. We both had shared our dreams of breaking
away from Uniontown's stagnant economy and moving
up in the world. Her good fortune inspired me to make
a change in my life too. I decided to go back to school. I
figured studying would keep me from thinking too much
about the mess my life had become.

One good thing that came out of my short time working for the newspaper was I discovered I could write well.
Growing up, I'd loved to write, and my essay papers were
always the ones chosen by the teacher to be read aloud in
class. When I was about fifteen, I started writing down
my childhood memories as they came to me, and found
the process to be cathartic. But I never realized I was a
good writer until, while working for the newspaper, I

began to garner praise from my boss for the feature stories I wrote. A community college in Henderson offered an associate's degree in journalism, and I thought that would be a good place to start.

I attained a government grant to pay my college tuition and a student loan to cover the rest. Dani drove me out to the college and helped me get signed up for all my classes. Everything seemed to be going smoothly—too smoothly for me—when it dawned on me I had a big problem that could stand in the way of me and my college degree: my driving phobia.

Because this irrational fear of mine embarrassed me so, I hadn't even told Dani about it. No one knew I got lost when I went to places I'd been dozens of times, like the grocery store and even work. I had to leave thirty minutes early whenever I went somewhere to allow for lost time. On my way to pick up the kids from Chad's, I'd be driving along fine when suddenly everything around me would turn foreign. Whenever this happened, I panicked, thinking I'd taken a wrong turn somewhere, and pulled into the first side road I saw to try to backtrack and figure out where I made my mistake. From there on, I took one wrong turn after another, until I found myself driving around in circles in a frenzy. Eventually I always made it to Chad's, but when I got there the kids were angry because I was late.

The thought of driving to Henderson every day was almost inconceivable to me. I needed help, and Dani was the only person I had to turn to. I didn't know what I expected her to do; I just thought she should know. In the car on our way back from the college, I inhaled a breath of gumption. "Dani, you know how I'm scared of water and heights?"

"Yeah?"

"There's something else I'm afraid of I haven't told you about."

She glanced over at me. "Really? What?"

"Driving; especially in a strange place, and sometimes if I'm in a lot of traffic and the cars around me are going fast."

"Huh. Well it's a good thing there's not much traffic where we live." She laughed. "Nobody gets in a hurry either."

"Actually, I'm more afraid of the getting lost part."

"That's funny; my mom is too!"

"She is?"

"Yep; she even gets lost in the Wal-Mart."

Hearing someone else had the same problem reminded me of when Aunt Macy took me to the doctor because I ate toilet paper, and he told me his sister ate chalk—like less of a freak. "She does?" I asked. "I get lost in the Wal-Mart too! And when I was a-kid I got lost in the school halls at least once a week."

"Mom's so bad she says when she's driving in a strange town and her mind tells her to turn one way, she turns the opposite."

"That works?"

"Does for her. But she's okay as long as she stays in Uniontown," She chuckled. "It's real hard to get lost there."

"No it isn't."

She looked at me incredulously. "You do? Still?"

"I've got it bad. It happens all the time; I just don't tell anybody."

"So what do you think your Mama did to you when you were a kid to bring this on?"

"I have no idea. I can't connect it to anything she did, unless it's because I don't have any confidence."

"Well don't worry, sweetie, I'll help you. If you need to go somewhere I'll write out directions."

"You don't understand, Dani. I have panic attacks when I drive. Sometimes I get physically ill and have to pull over."

"That bad, huh?"

"There's no way I can drive over thirty miles every day."

"Oh yes you can. You have to. Not only for college. If you ever plan on getting a decent job, you'll have to move somewhere else. Somewhere where there are a lot of cars that go fast."

"How am I going to do that when I can't even find my way around Uniontown?"

"I'll tell you how. I'm going to work with you until you're comfortable enough to drive to the college on your own. We'll start tomorrow."

The next afternoon Dani showed up at the front door of my apartment. "Let's go," she said, motioning for me to come outside. "Don't forget your car keys."

As soon as she said *car keys* my heart jolted. *She's serious.* "Where are the twins?" I asked.

"At Mom's. Hurry up, let's go. I told her I wouldn't be long."

I found my keys and we walked out to my Chevette together. Dani got in on the passenger side, and my heart jolted again. "You're going to tell me where to go, right?"

"Sure. The first few times, I will. But you need to learn to find your way on your own, because I won't be there when you drive to college."

Five miles outside of Uniontown, I had a panic attack and had to pull over and let Dani drive us back home. The second attempt was the same. The third and fourth attempts, I made it farther than before, but I still had to pull over and let Dani take the wheel when we got into traffic. Each time I tried to drive to school, I got a little farther without panicking, until one day I pulled into the college parking lot all by myself. We were both so excited, if either one of us had any money we would have thrown a party.

The real test came when fall classes started at the college. Dani drew me a map, and told me to pull over and call her if I needed to and she would talk me through it. Without Dani in the car with me, the first time I drove to the college I was terrified, but I made it. Of course I had to call her more than once, but knowing she was there and I was no longer alone with my secret made all the difference in the world.

Dani and I were at our favorite night club. She was out on the dance floor in a peacock blue dress that made her eyes pop out of the crowd like two sapphires on black silk. I'd had one too many of the tequila shots some nice guy with a lisp kept buying for me. Dani appeared to be having a good time dancing, and I didn't want to spoil the night by asking her to leave early, so I decided to go out to the car and crash in the backseat for a while.

Closing time rolled around, and Dani began searching for me in the club so we could leave. The last place she checked was a seating area upstairs. There was a cute guy up there sitting at a table by himself. "He's not up here," the guy said.

"He's a *she*," Dani said.

"Oh really. Well in that case let me help you find her." He joined Dani in her search for me, with no luck. When the dance club was empty and the employees were locking up, Dani figured I had to already be in the car. When she found me sleeping in the backseat, she pecked on the window to wake me. Through bleary eyes, I saw two moon-like faces, illuminated by street lights, looking down at me. Groggy, I sat up, opened the car door and climbed out, my dress hiking up in the process. Now aware that Dani had a guy with her, I tugged my dress back down as I stood up.

"This is Barry," Dani said, giving me the eye roll, her signal that she did not want to be with him.

One look at this poor guy's face and I knew he'd been mesmerized and lured in by Dani's large, freakishly blue eyes. "Hi Barry," I said.

Dani crinkled her nose and gritted her teeth. Her message couldn't have been clearer if she'd shouted, "For God's sake, Tuesday, help me lose this guy!"

I looked into Barry's puppy dog eyes. They were saying that whether I helped him or not, one way or the other, he was going to be with Dani. But I was Dani's best friend and my first loyalty was to her, and she wanted me to get rid of this joker.

In my stocking feet, I took a few steps forward and opened the passenger door of the car. "We're going to Denny's for breakfast, Barry," I said, as I got in. "Want to meet us there?"

"Sure! I'll follow you."

Barry walked off, and Dani stomped around the front of the car and got in behind the wheel. She always drove when we went out, not only because I was a lousy driver and could get lost in a box, but because she didn't drink—ever. When I asked her why, she wouldn't give me a direct answer, and I didn't press, but I figured she had her reasons.

"What was that all about?" Dani asked. "Didn't you get my signal? I don't like him."

"What's wrong with him? He's cute. Teddy bear cute."

"I don't know—he's... he's too nice. You know what I mean?"

"Too nice? That's the same thing you thought about me when I was trying to be your friend. Dani, just because someone is nice to you doesn't mean they're up to something. That ex of yours really did a number on your head."

"I'm not the only one in this car with trust issues."

"True. I guess it's easier to trust someone when my feelings aren't at risk." But I wasn't disregarding Dani's feelings. Somehow I knew Barry was a good guy, and when I looked at him I could see him in her future.

"You know the rule. If one of us has a guy hanging around at the end of the night, the other one helps her get rid of him. I thought we were supposed to look out for one another."

I am looking out for you; I thought. *You just don't know it yet.* "Hey, it's only breakfast," I said. "If you still don't like him by the time we've finished eating, don't give him your number. Or give him Pizza's King's number."

At Denny's, even before Dani had finished her toast and extra crispy bacon, she was writing a phone number on a paper napkin. And it wasn't Pizza King's.

The miracle I had been waiting for to end my relationship with Matt finally showed up. He was offered a job as center director of the Job Corps in Philadelphia. It was an offer he could not refuse, a major step up from his current position as head residential adviser.

What I had with Matt had never seemed real to me. It was like having a nice dream, but in the back of your mind you know you'll soon wake up. We played out the dream until the very end. He said he wanted me to come with him to Philadelphia. I told him to go ahead and find a place to live, and maybe I would join him one day. But we both knew that was never going to happen.

Dani was standing in the living room of my apartment, shifting her weight from one leg to the other. I could tell she was about to burst. She had called earlier and said she had a surprise. "We're getting married!" she shouted.

Why am I not surprised to hear this? "I'm so happy for you, honey!" I threw my arms around her. "Barry is a great guy!"

"I know; I'm so lucky."

"You *do* realize this would have never happened if I had listened to you that first night."

"I know, I know. I was wrong."

"And you know I'll never let you forget it. Twenty years from now I'll still be reminding you."

She smiled. We both knew we'd always be best friends. "We've decided to have a big church wedding." Dani said. "It's what I've always dreamed of."

"A big wedding takes a lot of planning."

"Are you kidding? I've been planning my wedding ever since I was a little girl!"

I laughed. "You *so* deserve this!"

"Of course you'll be my maid of honor."

"Of course!"

"Seriously, you're right. I've got so much planning to do. I'm going to be really busy."

"It'll be fun!"

"Have you decided when?"

"We were thinking July."

"That's less than six months from now! We'd better get started."

DARK TUESDAY

THE CHURCH WAS full of whispers as we waited for the bride to walk down the aisle. A combination of nerves, and the massive amount of satin I had on was causing me to perspire. I hated the dress Dani had chosen for me to wear. It was the typical maid of honor nightmare—teal green with sleeves so puffy they touched my cheeks when they weren't sliding off my shoulders from being so heavy. I told Dani I loved the dress. As her best friend, I was totally honest with her about everything, unless the truth would hurt her, or was something beyond her control. And the dress fit in to both categories. If I told her it was ugly she would surely be hurt, and it was all she could afford, which was beyond her control. What I looked like wasn't important anyway. This was Dani's day, the day she'd been dreaming of since she was a little girl.

With the first note of "Here Comes the Bride" tears began welling in my eyes. Somewhere under the yards upon yards of white satin, lace and tulle, was my sweet and loyal friend, who was also funny and smart and probably scared to death. Dani's marriage to Barry had many meanings. To Dani, it meant she would always be cherished by a good man. To her twins, whose biological father had all but disappeared from their lives, it meant they would now have a positive male role model. To Barry, marrying Dani meant he had found the woman of his dreams. To the rest of the teary-eyed people in the church, their marriage was proof that life really does go the way it's supposed to sometimes. To me, it meant I would no longer have Dani all to myself. No more nights out dancing, no more drinking three pots of coffee while talking into the wee hours of the morning.

Everything about the wedding turned out perfect—the bride, the ceremony, the vows, the twin ring bearers. As I watched the bride and groom exit the church on their way to their new life together, I was pretty sure Barry had no idea how lucky he was, but he would soon find out.

Business at the furniture store where I worked had slowed down, and the owner could no longer afford to pay me. He let me go and brought his wife in to take my place. Through the college, I got a minimum wage job as a night auditor for a motel in Henderson. Basically I issued rooms to truckers, and balanced the books before the manager came in at six in the morning. The hours allowed me to go to school during the day, but the money I made barely covered the rent on my one bedroom apartment. I had to scrape together change to put gas in the car, and I lived on four-for-a-dollar boxed macaroni and cheese that I prepared with water instead of milk.

Dani offered to let me stay in the basement of the house she and Barry had bought in Evansville. "It will only be until you get your degree and find a full time job," she said. But I felt like a freeloader now that she was married. I insisted on paying them something and they finally agreed to take seventy-five dollars a month if it would make me feel better.

Living in a basement with no sunlight went along with the gloomy moods that had begun to take hold of me. When Dani asked me what was wrong, I couldn't say exactly why I felt so low, only that I had an ever-present, dull emotional ache.

It had become more difficult to pry Molly and Daryl away from their friends to spend time with me, especially Molly who was now a teenager. When I picked them up from Chad's, I struggled to engage them in conversation in the car. I could tell they would rather be doing something else. Coming to my dingy basement room seemed like a chore to them.

Around this time, my younger brother, Ryan, called to tell me he wanted to talk about our childhood. He said he was curious because he hardly remembered me at all growing up. He told me he knew something bad must have occurred concerning me, because I had left home at such an early age. He wanted to know what it was.

Because I had been isolated from my brothers as a child, in the more than twenty years since I left home, I'd had no motivation to reconnect with them. They were like

acquaintances to me, nice people I had met—one of them
I could even say had once been a casual friend. But when
you lose contact with acquaintances and casual friends
it's easy to forget all about them once they're out of your
sight. What normally makes us miss our family, makes
us want to see them—a shared history of precious childhood memories—was the essential element absent in my
relationship with my brothers. And if the presence of that
void wasn't enough to keep us apart, the fear that the
dreaded subject might come up in conversation, dredg-
ing up our unresolved pain and guilt, was sure to make
us want to put as much space between us as possible.

Barry was anxious to meet Ryan. Dani already knew
him from school, but they hadn't actually met. I wanted
Barry and Dani both to be present when Ryan and I
talked, because I was nervous about our meeting and
needed their support. They had become my family, and
like I had told Ryan over the phone, I had no secrets from
them.

Ryan looked nothing like the scrawny, towheaded
boy I'd seen in the pictures Daddy had given me. He was
tall and lanky like Daddy with an Irish face like Mama's.
He was in college, beginning his life as an adult. Almost
immediately after I had introduced him to Barry and
Dani, he said to them, "I want you both to know I can't
remember any of what happened; I must have blocked it
out of my memory."

Blocked it out? Hmm, wonder where he got that?

He wanted to know what happened, so I told him
a generalized version of the abuse Mama had inflicted

upon me. Afterward, he stuck to his story that he couldn't remember any of what I had revealed. I doubted he was being completely truthful. He'd been older—five or six—when most of the worst of my abuse went on. He probably had struggled with disturbing memories—albeit fuzzy, given his age—that when they surfaced caused conflicting emotions, so he had *pushed* them from his mind. Looking back as a man, he may have felt guilty for not telling anyone what was happening to his sister, but as a child, he was as helpless and innocent as I was.

He didn't say, but I knew what he thought. He thought because I'd been the only one, Mama's negative treatment of me had to be the result of something I'd done. He wanted me to be the bad one, not the mother he adored. How could he continue to love someone capable of such cruelty? And I was willing to allow him to walk away with those beliefs, because I didn't care. I just wanted him to go away and leave me alone.

As soon as he was out the door, Dani said she didn't buy Ryan's claim to have forgotten only selected parts of his childhood. "He has to remember *something*," she said. "If he doesn't then how does he even know there's anything to block out in the first place? People don't block out good memories." I agreed with her, but had no desire to make things right, or forge a relationship with Ryan. And he, in turn, had no intention of having anything further to do with me. He had done what he'd come to do—to exonerate himself. Watching him drive away, I knew I would not see him again until someone in the family died.

As soon as I got my associates degree in journalism, I put in job applications at several local newspapers, but every place I tried was cutting back instead of hiring. The only other skill I had to offer an employer was in retail. I decided to pass up the mall, and apply at a few of the furniture stores in Evansville, because I knew I would make more money there, and maybe even get some insurance.

I got on at a furniture store near Dani's house, and rented an apartment nearby, because I was fairly comfortable driving in that area. Aside from picking up the kids, I drove to Dani's, work, and the grocery store. I still got lost once in a while, but Dani was always a phone call away to bail me out.

Shortly after I moved to Evansville, I began going through the motions of life only as necessity dictated to me. Living had become a reflex, a physical function over which I had no control, but I was far from being alive. To fit in at my new job, I socialized with co-workers, but I wouldn't allow myself to become close to anyone. When I went home at the end of the day, I never wanted to call the people with whom I worked, or invite them over. I looked upon those who did crave this sort of close and constant human contact with bewilderment. I had enough common sense to know such detachment was not normal, so I went to great lengths to conceal this part of myself from co-workers, my children, and Dani. Since I'd gotten into the habit of switching my own emotions off, I studied how other people reacted to various situations and learned how to mimic them.

Despite my overall anti-social behavior, for some reason, I thought I should always have a man in my life, and somehow, I always managed to have one. Judging by what I saw in the mirror, I could never understand why they were attracted to me. Dani said it was because I was blond, had "legs that went forever" and a warm southern way about me.

Mostly I dated my parents—submissive, subservient types, like my father, or men who were domineering and controlling, ebbing on abusive, like my mother. Some of these men rushed headlong into my life, others I handpicked and then lured in, but each of them was carefully qualified by me to help me along the self-destructive path I had begun to travel.

The controlling and possessive men made me feel wanted and loved—a familiar and dangerously comfortable place for me to be. The worse they treated me, tried to dominate me, the more I clung to them, seeking their approval. I drew these partners into my life in a pathetic effort to re-enact the abusive patterns of my childhood. In my misguided psyche, I thought by recreating my past, maybe I could somehow gain my mother's love through these men.

Whenever a loving, sensitive man, with whom I could possibly build a stable future stumbled into my path, I managed to find a way to run him off, or sabotage the relationship in order to fulfill my masochistic prophecy of a life doomed to suffering and isolation—the only life of which my mother had convinced me I deserved. Years of her hammering away at my self-esteem had made me feel unworthy of this level of affection, and so I didn't allow myself to accept it.

As a child, all I wanted was to be loved. As an adult, all I wanted was to be loved. But it was hard for me to believe in happily ever after when the one person I should have been able to count on to love me unconditionally had failed me. If my own mother didn't think I was deserving of love, how could I expect anyone else to? The thought of having my heart mutilated again scared the hell out of me, so to retain a sense of safety, I always kept a part of it to myself, hidden and protected. Because I never allowed anyone too close, or trusted anyone enough to give up my heart, I'd been unable to develop healthy, long-term relationships.

My mother wasn't all to blame. Because of Daddy, I saw men as being weak, untrustworthy creatures that could be easily manipulated. My father's betrayal was like an earthquake to my soul, and every time thereafter when another man came along and in some way betrayed me, I felt the aftershock.

Even though I had trouble developing lasting relationships with men, I still dreamed the dream. Whenever I thought I was in love, I went through all the motions, playing out the love stories I'd read about, or seen at the movies, sometimes at the expense of some poor man's heart. I never did this maliciously—each time I believed my feelings were real. But, as it always turned out, being in love was a brilliant star far beyond my reach.

DESCENT

AT THREE O'CLOCK in the morning, I was sitting in the dark, on the kitchen floor of my apartment, eating vanilla wafers from the box. The night before, I'd sat in the same spot, at the exact time, shoving sour cream and onion potato chips into my mouth by the handfuls. The night before that, I'd eaten a whole jar of peanut butter and half a sack of marshmallows.

My bizarre eating habit had been going on for months. Every morning, at three o'clock, give or take a few minutes, my eyes snapped open, I rose from my bed, and like a zombie, plodded into the kitchen and ate the first thing I could get my hands on. I never turned on the light, as if eating in the dark somehow made it less real. I sat on the floor, as if by not sitting at the table I could fool myself into thinking I was not actually eating. But I was eating, and fully awake and well aware of what I was doing. I knew, and yet I still couldn't stop.

It wasn't hard to figure out why I'd started eating in the middle of the night. Hunger had been a constant in my childhood, and now, as an adult, food remained significant in my life. When I was a child, Mama had withheld food from me to the point where I finally found the courage to sneak out of bed while the rest of the family slept and steal something to eat from the kitchen. So it was no surprise that I'd begun reliving this pattern, and like when I was a child, eating and eating, unable to satisfy my hunger. But I couldn't understand why it was happening at this particular point in my life. Had I pushed my past away one time too many, and now it was pushing back?

In addition to the middle of the night eating, my tendency to inertia, and my unhealthy desire for isolation had begun to overwhelm me. Being alone at the end of my work day had become as soothing and comforting as a cup of cocoa on a cold night. But that's the danger of isolation; it lures you in with the deceptive promise of protecting you and then it feasts on your spirit. Becoming a recluse would have been my preferred way to live, but I couldn't because of my children, and the necessity of a job that forced me to interact with people, the despicable creatures I didn't entirely trust. But if I didn't go to work I didn't eat. And I had to eat. I *had* to eat, because I was a damn cockroach, a survivor, even if I didn't want to be.

I'd always been efficient at activating the protective mechanism of shutting off my feelings whenever I felt threatened. The problem had now become, lately, I always felt threatened. Each day, I turned more and more reclusive, retreating within myself, going out only when necessary, calling in sick for work or showing up late.

Even when I was at my job, I wasn't. My sales had plummeted, and it had become a daily challenge to conceal my true self from co-workers. As soon as I got home every day, I collapsed on the sofa, drained from having held up such a heavy façade. I was afraid if I couldn't somehow gain the capacity to effectively bond with other people, I'd reach the point where I would no longer be able to function in society.

The many blessings in my life were getting lost in the dense, gray fog of my depression. I'd become distant and emotionally unavailable to my children, tangled in the underbrush of the mental anguish caused by my own self-induced isolation. Molly and Daryl had always saved me before. Whenever I slipped into my black hole, loving them, caring for them, had brought me back out. But there was no saving me now. This time I had sunk too far—was still sinking—and I knew dragging my children down with me would be the cruelest thing I could ever do to them.

The time I wasn't at work I spent in bed with the curtains drawn. I was afraid of what the light might expose. I got to where I wouldn't answer the phone. Whenever it rang, I cringed and covered my ears, but I couldn't bring myself to pick up the receiver and stop the ringing. Like my fear of driving, I couldn't connect my phone phobia with anything from my childhood. I simply added it to the long list of my other fears.

Some days I didn't bother to get dressed, bathe, or brush my teeth. I was too exhausted for hygiene, exhausted from years of smiling, hiding, fighting—surviving. Mama had finally made good on her threat to throw me into a bottomless pit; I was spinning downward fast and nothing could stop me, not Dani, not even my kids.

I began concocting excuses for not getting the kids on the weekends, because I didn't want them to see me in such a state. I had reached the bitter and shameful realization that Molly and Daryl were better off with Chad. On some level, I'd always known I would inevitably end up in a dark place. The eating disorder, the endless string of obsessions, had all been a preview of the big show to come. Even the nature of my marriage to Chad should have sent up a red flag. Only a woman with no confidence or sense of self-worth would have allowed a man to dominate her in such a way.

Fleeting thoughts of suicide began passing through my head. The first time it happened, I was soaking in the bathtub; the water was warm and beckoning, caressing my shoulders like a lover easing me into his bed. Reflected in the milky water, I could see the glaring overhead light and white tiled walls of the bathroom. Even the curve of my leg, propped up on the ledge of the soap tray, was perfectly replicated. The world in the water was identical to the world in which I lived, but without the hard, hard edges. With every drop from the leaky faucet, the watery world rippled softly. *It's a more malleable world,* I thought. *One I can possibly change. Fix.*

That's when it came to me—a fraction of a second when I believed maybe I could do it, slide under, head and all. Take a deep breath. Slowly I dropped my leg, allowing my body to ease into the tub. As soon as the water wrapped around my neck, warm like a gloved-hand, I remembered Mama's grip as she smashed my face into the bottom of the bathtub, and jolted up, gasping for air—the same thing I always did whenever water came within inches of my face. *What was I thinking? Hell, I can't even drink a glass of water without losing my breath.*

My first flirt with death had only been a notion, I told myself, a moment of impulse. *A lot of people think about killing themselves with no intentions of actually doing it.* But then the thoughts began to visit me more frequently. I began thinking in detail, considering the different options of suicide, most of which were not available to me, because I was afraid of almost everything. Obviously water was out of the question. I couldn't bear the sight of blood, and I had a paralyzing fear of heights. So right away, I could eliminate jumping off a bridge and slitting my wrists. I considered an overdose of pills, but decided it was not a reliable solution. I'd seen too many people on TV who'd been found in a stupor from an overdose and ended up in the hospital getting a stomach pump.

After careful consideration, I chose carbon monoxide poisoning. I'd read somewhere it was the most painless way to go. *Who needs more pain?* Sitting in a dusky car with the motor running, drifting peacefully to my death, seemed movie-star glamorous, in a morbid sort of way. In the movies, people who killed themselves with carbon monoxide usually did it in a garage. I didn't have a garage, but Dani did, and she and Barry were taking a vacation soon. They always asked me to watch their house whenever they went out of town. It would be the perfect opportunity. The plan had been made. The time had been set.

Standing in the checkout line at the Wal-Mart, I went over my mental checklist to make sure I had everything I needed: *a water hose, a roll of duct tape, and a box of Sominex.* My next stop would be the liquor store, where I'd buy the most expensive champagne I could find, and then I'd fill the gas tank of my car before driving to Dani's house. When there was only one person in line in front of me, the checker glanced at the contents of my shopping cart. I began to get paranoid. *Does she suspect something?*

I'd always hated people who committed suicide hated them for wimping out on life, leaving their loved ones behind with shattered hearts and unanswered questions. But death seemed like the only escape from the hopelessness that had consumed me. I hated myself for needing to escape, for my weakness. *After all I've overcome I'm giving up now? How can I do this to my children on top of what I've already put them through? How can I do it to Dani ?* I imagined how devastated she would be coming home from her vacation to find her best friend dead in her garage. I turned my shopping cart around, excused myself through the line of people behind me, and headed for the exit. When I got to the door, I abandoned my cart and ran out of the store. I needed help and I needed it fast.

Close by where I lived, there was a state mental hospital with a lovely pond beside it, and I decided to swing by the apartment to pick up some stale bread, and then go there and feed the ducks. It was a place where I felt at peace, and in my heart I knew it was where I belonged.

As I sat on the bank of the pond, tossing bread crumbs to eager ducks, I watched the patients wander mindlessly about the grounds of the hospital, and longed to join them—join *my people*. I wanted to stand in line every day for a pill—a pill to make me forget the past, make me numb to the future. That's when something dawned on me: *Maybe I can get such a pill.*

When I got home, I called and made an appointment with the only doctor I'd seen in years, the same one who had delivered Molly and Daryl.

My thoughts were all over the place as I sat waiting for Dr. Watson to come in. My elbows were locked at my side, palms pressed flat against the thin sheet of paper beneath me, and my legs hung stiffly over the edge of the examination table, like two icicles. *What will I say? How much should I tell him? What the hell am I doing in here?*

There was nothing to be afraid of. I'd known Dr. Watson for*ever*, and in the most personal way. I should have been able to tell the man anything. But suddenly, spreading my legs and baring my bald vagina, while pushing out a seven pound baby seemed far less revealing than what I was about to do.

I thought of the first time I'd seen him. I'd been throwing up for weeks. "You're pregnant," he'd said, barely glancing at me. "But for formality's sake, I'll do the test."

Then there was the time, six months into my pregnancy, when I was still throwing up at least twice a day.

"I can't keep anything down, Dr. Watson," I whined.

He looked at me with steely gray eyes. "Like Popsicles?" he asked. He always responded with short, snippy sentences, like he was in a hurry. This might have offended some people, but I liked that he never tried to poke around in my life.

"Yes, I like Popsicles."

"Suck on Popsicles then."

And how could I forget the day I went into labor with Molly? After fifteen hours of screaming profanities at Chad and hallucinating from pain medication, Dr. Watson walked in my hospital room, dragging a bum leg he'd gotten from a war wound. After he'd examined me, he patted me on the hip and said, "You've got a long way to go, missy. See you tomorrow."

The door to the examination room opened, and Dr. Watson slid in sideways. "What's the problem?" he asked, peering up over his glasses at me.

"I've been exhausted lately, Dr. Watson. Some days I don't even want to get out of bed." I took a deep breath. "And... and..." Then I started crying, blubbering like a fool, until I could no longer form words.

"You need an anti-depressant?" he asked.

"Yes... I mean, do *you* think I do?"

"Sounds like it. The thing with anti-depressants is they mess up your sex life."

Sex was the last thing on my mind. "I can deal with that."

He cracked a brief smile. "You're still young. You might not feel that way after your mood picks up." He studied me for a minute. "There is one that might work well for you. It has the least sexual side-effects, and it'll get you out of bed."

"Anything," I blurted.

He jotted something on his prescription pad. "You'll have to take it twice a day, as soon as your feet hit the floor in the morning, and again around two in the afternoon."

When I got home with the prescription, I opened the bottle and poured the pills out into my hand. Purple tablets—not what I expected. I thought they would be more interesting, maybe shiny red or yellow capsules, like in the movies. I took one immediately.

I didn't know what to expect from the pills Dr. Watson had prescribed. I'd read somewhere that anti-depressants turned people into zombies incapable of experiencing essential human emotion. But I figured I had nothing to lose by taking them, because I was already an emotionless zombie. I followed the prescription religiously. A week went by, and I felt the same as before. After two weeks, still nothing. Then right around the third or fourth week, I started to notice an improvement in my mood.

After two months of taking the medication twice a day, every day, my outlook on life changed radically. I bounced out of bed in the mornings ready to tackle the day ahead of me. I opened the curtains in my bedroom and plugged the phone back in. I looked forward to seeing my children, and even started going out to dinner with co-workers. As an added bonus, I no longer had the urge to smoke, or the compulsion to get up in the night and stuff myself with food. And the eating disorder I'd been trying to keep at bay for years, practically disappeared overnight. Later, I discovered this particular drug was commonly used to help people quit smoking, and sometimes to treat anorexia. The difference was palpable, and the fact clear: I needed the purple happy pills to function, just as diabetics need insulin.

PUSHING OFF THE BOTTOM

ONE AFTERNOON, ON her way home from work, Dani stopped by my apartment, grinning like a kid who'd discovered an M&M tree growing in her backyard. "You've got to read this," she said, extending a thin book to me. "Tonight."

I took the book from her and read the title. "A Child Called "It." What's it about?"

You're not going to believe this, but the man who wrote this book went through almost the *exact* same thing you did when you were a kid."

"What? No way."

"I'm serious—read it, you'll see."

Overcome with curiosity, I started reading the book as soon as she left. From page one, I became enthralled with the author's heart-wrenching account of his severe childhood abuse. Dani was right, the similarities in our stories were startling. Not only had the author been severely beaten and starved by his mother, just as I was; he was also the only child in the family singled out to be treated this way. Both of our fathers were passive and did hardly anything to help our situations, and the jaw-dropping part was there were so many parallels in the details of the systematic, often twisted behavior of both our mothers. For instance, both of us were not allowed to look at anyone in our families, and neither one of our mothers would call us by our names. His mother referred to him as "it," or "the boy" and mine called me "weasel," or "horse face."

Our mothers were so similar, they could have been sisters, and after I had read *A Child Called "It"* I felt as though I had found a brother in the author. I wanted to write him a letter to thank him for sharing his story, and tell him he'd made a huge difference in at least one person's life. I wanted to let him know how brave I thought he was for writing about all the degrading things his mother had done to him, for finding the courage to write his story, regardless of how his family might react, and that people might doubt the validity. And I had a question to ask him, too, the same question that had been gnawing at my brain for years. I wanted to know if he had any idea why we were the only ones targeted for abuse. I searched everywhere on the internet but couldn't find a way to contact him directly.

I had to talk to somebody, so I called Dani. "Put on a pot of coffee," I said "I'm coming over."

Dani looked at me over her cup of coffee. "You should

write a book about your childhood," she said. "You're a great writer."

"But I can't write a *book*."

"Yes you can. You thought you couldn't drive to Henderson either, but you did."

"I'm afraid if I wrote a book some people would be embarrassed."

"Like who?"

"Like my brothers."

"When have your brothers ever cared about you and the hell you went through? You're right; it may embarrass them to read the details of what your mother did to you. I'm sure they love her because she never mistreated them. But I'll bet your story helps more people than it hurts."

"I think two of my brothers have kids, not to mention Molly and Daryl—that's their *grandmother*."

"As far as your kids go, your mother has never been a part of their lives. And your brothers will have to deal with their kids in their own way. You have a right to tell your story. It was all kept quiet to protect the family for too long. Now it's your turn to talk."

"The rest of my family, and maybe some neighbors, might also be offended because they did nothing to help me."

"Who cares? Besides, it's not about your family; it's about you and the many people who will gain inspiration from your story. Look, if you're so worried about your family then change all the names. Authors do it all the time. Just get your story out there. That way your suffering will not have been for nothing."

"They'll probably deny it, you know."

"Of course they will. No one wants to admit to having any part in something like that. Or, who knows? They might surprise you. Most of them didn't know how bad it was for you. Maybe deep down they want to know, maybe they *need* to know."

"What if nobody believes me?"

"The people who matter will believe you." She sat her coffee down. "I know what you're afraid of. You're afraid that what happened with social services when you were a kid will happen again. But I can tell you this: it never once occurred to me while you were telling me your story that what you were saying wasn't true. I could feel the pain in your words and see it in your eyes."

"I don't know if I *can* write about everything that happened to me, all the disgusting things I had to do. Maybe *I'm* embarrassed."

"Tuesday, you're not giving the readers enough credit. Most people are compassionate. They'll get it!"

"You think?"

"Let me ask you something. How did you feel while you were reading *A Child Called It?*"

"Inspired, and this may sound awful, but also a little glad I wasn't the only one."

"Do you doubt it's true?"

"No! I *know* it's true, because the same thing happened to me!"

"Look, I'm not going to push you on this, because we've been there before, and I know if I push you you'll run the other way. I want to say one more thing, and then

I'll drop it. I feel strongly about you writing this book—getting it all out, dealing with what happened on your own terms, and I'm not going to let you forget about it. You have a story that needs to be told, and you're a gifted writer. How many more hints does Fate have to give you?"

"Okay, you're right. I'll write a book—someday."

Dani dropped the subject, like she said she would, but she never let me forget about what came to be known between us as "the book." She continued to slip it into conversation from time to time, address, and shoot down all my excuses, then back off again.

SEARCHING FOR THE SURFACE

WE NEVER KNOW when someone special is going to walk into our life. Someone who, if we don't flub things up, could play a significant role in our future. Had I known ahead of time such a person was coming my way I would've been better prepared. I would've worn a more flattering dress, spent more time on my hair that morning, and thought up some cool lines to make me seem clever and confident. But I didn't know he was coming, so I was left with no other choice than to be me, the awkward, insecure me, who wasn't confident or cool, or beautiful, even on a good hair day.

About ten minutes before closing at the furniture store, a fortyish man came in and zipped past the counter. He was the customer all salespeople hate. The one who comes in right before a store closes, most likely intentionally, knowing he'll be free to browse in peace, because no salesperson wants to deal with a customer ten minutes before closing time.

From my now extensive experience in sales, I'd found

that if I left such a customer alone, he sometimes stayed past closing, but if I played the part of the typical pesky salesperson and followed him around the store every step he took, I'd chase him right back out the door.

I got on the customer's heels and followed him to the bedding department at the back of the store. As soon as he got there, he sat down on the most expensive pillow-top mattress we sold. The salesperson in me became excited. In addition to commission, I received a healthy spiff from the manufacturer every time I sold that particular mattress. But before I launched my sales spiel, I reminded myself that the right-before-closing customer usually didn't buy.

But what if this guy's different? What if he needs a mattress now? I couldn't risk losing a good sale. "So you need a mattress?" I said, trying not to sound too anxious. "The one you're on would be an excellent choice."

He looked at me with watercolor blue eyes.

"Is this one the best you sell?" he asked.

"Top of the line."

He smiled. Although he was middle-aged, evident by his slightly thinning hair, he had an impish smile, giving him a child-like quality. "I'll take it then, in king size."

Wow that was easy. "Are you sure? No one else has to try it out?"

"Nope; only me."

Divorced; she got the furniture. "Well in that case, come with me and I'll write it up for you."

"How soon can you deliver?" he asked, as we approached the front desk.

"We have the bedding in stock, so we can have it to you within the next few days. By the way, there's no delivery fee on our bedding."

"Excellent!"

"I just need to get some information from you," I said. Darla, another saleswoman who was behind the counter, gave me a surprised smirk when I picked up a sales ticket. "Your name, sir?"

"Colin Scott."

Two first names; Grandma Storm once told me to never trust anyone with two first names. Hope he doesn't write a bad check. "And your address?"

"Ridgeway Apartments, apartment twenty."

Definitely divorced. "And we'll need your phone number so our delivery crew can call and tell you when they'll be bringing your mattress."

He pulled a business card from his wallet. "Here's my card. They can call me at my office, and I'll leave work and meet them at the apartment. It's only five minutes away."

"*Dr.* Colin Scott?" I read aloud from the card.

"You're a doctor?" Darla asked. "I've been looking for a good doctor."

"You should call the office and make an appointment," he said, handing Darla a card. Then he turned to me. "What about you... I'm sorry I didn't get your name..."

"Tuesday."

"Do you need a doctor, Tuesday?"

"Well, I don't have one in Evansville yet. Maybe."

He smiled. "Do you have a business card, Tuesday? I need an entire bedroom suite, but I'll come back at another time for that."

He took my card, paid for his mattress, and then left the store. As Darla was locking up behind him, she giggled and said, "I think he likes you."

"What makes you say that?"

"The way he looked at you when you weren't paying attention. And all the grinning. I've never seen anyone that happy about buying a mattress."

"Oh, he was just being nice. And maybe trying to drum up patients. Besides, he's a doctor. Why would a doctor be interested in me?"

"Why wouldn't he? Look at you!"

"You're sweet, Darla; but I don't think so."

That night, when I got home, I stood in front of my mirror thinking about what Darla had said. I saw blotchy skin, still prone to regular breakouts, stringy, blond hair and a nose noticeably crooked from being broken more than once. I saw a mouth that simply refused to smile without considerable effort, which sometimes gave my face a forlorn haggard appearance. Stepping back, I twisted my hair into a bun at my crown, did a quarter turn of my head, and faked a smile. I knew there was no possible way a man like Colin could be interested in the woman I saw in the mirror. Doctors go out with pretty women from good families with masters degrees from reputable colleges, or women so gorgeous intelligence doesn't matter. Or nurses—perky fresh-out-of-college nurses. Not a mousy salesclerk with a screwed up past, who'd recently been teetering on the edge of sanity. Such things don't happen—ever—not even in the movies. I dropped my hair—and my smile—and went to bed.

Molly, now fifteen, had grown into a striking young lady with a wholesome, girl next door quality. She wore hardly any make-up because she didn't need to. Her cheeks were already blushed; her skin smooth and even, and her eyelashes naturally thick and dark. She wore her shiny black-brown hair in a straight, simple style, and often pulled it back in a high ponytail. She was dating now, all wrapped up in a steady boyfriend, and so she had little time for Chad or me.

Daryl, taking after my side of the family, was blond and lanky-tall, bearing a vague resemblance to Jimmy D. He too always seemed to be busy doing something with his friends. He hated coming to Evansville. The times I was able to coax him into staying with me, all he wanted to do was go to the mall. When we were there, he walked five steps either in front of, or behind me, but never by my side where I wanted him. He'd reached a stage where being seen hanging out with his mom was a threat to his cool factor. I understood, but his new attitude broke my heart, because I still saw him as a toddler with his arms wrapped around my leg.

With my head now bobbing up from the deep end of my depression, I yearned to reconnect with Aunt Macy. I called the only number I had for her, but it had been disconnected. Information had a listing under Edwin's name, so I dialed it.

Edwin picked up the phone."Edwin? This is Tuesday, Macy's niece. Do you remember me?"

"Yes, of course. How are you?"

"Well, I'm divorced now, and life's been a bit rough lately. That's why I haven't tried to contact Aunt Macy in a while. But things are better now. The kids are healthy, and so am I. I guess I can't complain."

"Sorry to hear you've been having trouble."

"Oh, don't be. Everything's fine. Could I talk to Aunt Macy? I'm anxious to catch up."

"Oh, I'm afraid that's not possible, Tuesday."

"Why?"

"Macy has been very ill, and part of her illness is that she can't communicate. She tries to talk, but nothing comes out. I think she's a bit confused in her head, and she's afraid if she says anything she'll embarrass herself."

"What's the nature of her illness?"

"At first the doctor said her problems were hormonal, so he prescribed some medication, and it seemed to help for a while. Then one day she stopped talking. I thought maybe it was a side effect of the medication, so I took her back to the doctor. She's on another medication now, but there's been no improvement. They have been running test after test on her, but they just can't seem to figure out what it is."

"Does she have any other symptoms?"

"Just general malaise; she has no energy, or will to go out. She's lost her spirit, Tuesday."

"Would you tell her I called and when she feels better to call me?"

"Yes, but I wouldn't expect her to for a while."

"Should I come to see her?"

"No, no, she won't see anyone."

"She'll see *me*."

"No she won't. She knows I'm on the phone with you now and she's shaking her head *no*."

"She doesn't want to see me?"

"I think she doesn't want you to see her as she is. She has the Storm pride, you know."

"Will you hold the phone up to her ear so I can tell her something?"

"I guess I can do that."

"Aunt Macy, I love you so much, and I miss you, and I'm sorry I didn't listen to you when you tried to help me. But I want you to know I went to school and got my degree and..."

Edwin got back on the phone. "Tuesday, I'm going to have to hang up, now. Something you said has made Macy anxious and she's started to cry."

"Will you tell her I'll call back in a few weeks to see if she's better?"

"I'll be sure to do that, Tuesday. Take care," he said, and hung up the phone.

I waited a week and called again. This time no one answered. For weeks, I kept calling but no one ever picked up. It occurred to me that Edwin might not have had caller ID on his phone, and I hadn't given him a number where Aunt Macy could reach me. I sent my number in a letter to the address I got from the phone book, and never got a response. I sent another letter in case she didn't get the first one. All of my letters went unanswered.

The cute doctor who bought the mattress came back into the furniture store and ordered a high end bedroom suite. He was sweet and smiley, like before, but also like before, he didn't act the least bit interested in me. *Silly Darla,* I thought. Still he seemed like a nice guy. I told him I liked to do business with people who did business with me, and when I needed a doctor I would be sure to call him.

Later on that day, Darla paged me to the phone. "It's Colin Scott, that doctor," she said. "I told you he liked you."

"He doesn't like me, Darla. He ordered a bedroom suite and he's probably wanting to add a nightstand or something. I pulled Colin's information up on the computer, and then picked up the phone. "Hello Colin, how can I help you?"

"I'm not calling about furniture," he said. "I'm calling about something else."

Could it be? "What is it, then, Colin?"

"Well, Darla called the office this morning and made an appointment. When I got home this afternoon, it hit me that you might want to do the same."

Oh, crap; he's trying to get me to be a patient again. This guy must be a lousy doctor to have to solicit patients to this extent...

"I don't want you to be my patient, because if you're

my patient I can't go out with you, and I want to go out with you. That is, if you will." He paused a second or two, and then said, "Tuesday, life is full of missed opportunities and I don't want to miss the opportunity to get to know you better."

"So you're asking me for a date?"

"Yes, a date. With me."

After I told him I'd go out with him, I wished I hadn't. When I hung up, I wanted to call him right back and tell him I'd changed my mind, but decided to call Dani instead.

"Dani, I've got this huge problem," I said. "You're not going to believe this, but the cute guy I was telling you about..."

"The divorced guy who bought the expensive mattress?"

"Yeah, that's the one. Anyway, he just called and asked me out to dinner!"

"So, the problem is...?"

"The *problem* is I can't go out with him!"

"Why?"

"Why do you think? Because he's a *doctor!*"

"And you're going to hold that against him?" Dani had the patience of a saint. She had twin boys—hyperactive twin boys. She'd sat through my six failed attempts to drive to the college on my own and never said a word. She hardly ever got agitated with me, but there was definitely agitation in her voice now. "You told me about this guy's dreamy eyes and sweet smile before you even mentioned he was a doctor, which means you were attracted to him *before* you found out what he did for a living, right?"

"He's *so* nice; a real gentleman."

"What if he didn't ask you out because you're a sales-clerk, a job some may consider inferior to his profession?"

"I'd think he was an arrogant snob."

"But he's not a snob! You will be though—sort of... in reverse—if you won't go out with him because of what he does for a living."

"You're right; he can't help it if he's a doctor."

"No, he can't. You like this guy, and obviously he likes you, so go out with him and forget he's a doctor."

"Gosh, I don't know if I can do *that*."

"Well try, When's your date?"

"Friday night."

"This Friday? Wow that's three days away."

"I'll have to have a new outfit."

"Of course you will; we'll go shopping tomorrow."

Somehow I found the confidence to go out with Colin. He was charming and attentive on our date, and confessed to being just as nervous as I was.

He asked me out again, and soon we became a couple, spending practically every day together. Molly and Daryl liked him, and he had two young daughters I was crazy about. No one had ever treated me as well as Colin did. He never talked down to me, or made me feel inferior in any way, and he acted proud to have me by his side during pharmaceutical events and dinners with his brainy colleagues. He was not the least bit jealous or possessive. The problem was I was used to jealous and possessive. Jealous and possessive felt like love to me, or what I thought love felt like.

After we had been dating for several months, Colin suggested we get a place and move in together. We rented a beautiful furnished house in a golfing community overlooking the eighteenth hole. The house was spacious, and there was a bedroom for each of our kids. Molly and Daryl liked it better than any other place we'd lived since the divorce, and they started visiting more. The house—contemporary and decorated in colors of taupe, beige, and ecru—had soaring windows, a winding staircase, and an indoor koi pond. I couldn't help but chuckle when I thought of the miniscule trailer I'd once been content to live in, with its orange shag carpet and holes in the paneled walls. *Life is truly unpredictable,* I thought. *And it has a sense of humor too.*

Everything about my relationship with Colin appeared perfect on the exterior. At times, it even felt perfect. Still, skulking in the back alleys of my mind was my fear of rejection. Fear that Colin would someday cast me aside like Daddy had, because I wasn't good enough.

When I thought the time was right, I decided to include Colin in the handful of people I'd trusted with the secret of my past. I didn't go into detail; I simply told him I had been an abused child. He was gentle, supportive and sympathetic. I thought sharing this intimate secret with him would bring us closer, but instead it did the opposite. Either he told his ex-wife about my history of abuse, or he told his girls and they told her. However she found out, she knew, and sent word through Colin that she didn't want her children around someone who was potentially unstable.

Hearing this, cut to the bone. Not that it was something I hadn't heard before. The prisons and mental hospitals are full of proof that child abuse victims can be wacko. But I loved Colin's girls and enjoyed being around them. They helped to fill the void when my own kids weren't around. Colin assured me he had no intention of keeping his kids away from me, but he thought I should know in case the girls mentioned it. He held up to his promise, but after that incident things were never quite the same between us.

In the spring of our second year together, we took a vacation to Hawaii. Sharing with Colin, the magic of Maui's waterfalls spilling into shimmering turquoise water was so romantic it almost fooled me into believing I'd be with him forever. And then I boarded the plane back to reality.

Not long after we returned from our trip, he stopped by my work, all excited. "I bought a condo!" he said, his boyish grin overtaking his face. "I just came from signing the papers!"

Colin and I had been living together for over six months. We were a couple. We did everything together, and yet he had bought a condo without telling me? After all, I was going to live there too, wasn't I? Granted he was paying for the condo, and therefore would have had the last say, but he could have humored me by asking me to go along with him to look at it, like he did when we rented the house. He could have at least made me think I had a voice in the matter.

"You bought a condo without telling me?" I asked. "Why did you do that, Colin? I didn't even know you were looking for a place!"

"I wanted to surprise you. I thought you would be excited, like me," he said. "I know it's sudden, but I decided to go ahead and act because it was such a good deal, and I knew the minute I walked in it was exactly what I wanted. You're going to love it, too, honey. I can't wait for you to see it! It has a pool and a sauna, and a theater room with a wet bar!"

Exactly what *he* wanted? "How much did you have to pay for it?"

"Under three hundred thousand."

"That's a good deal? It seems like a lot of money for a condominium."

"But it's not your typical condo. You'll just have to see it; it's worth every penny."

I had to tend to a customer, and Colin had to get back to work too. We agreed to talk more about it later.

To me, buying the condo was his way of separating us, of letting me know I didn't have a say in what he chose to do with his life, and that his future did not include me—he just hadn't found a way to break it to me yet. But of course I saw it that way. I had spent the entire relationship wondering why he was with me, waiting for the big dump, convinced I was merely a temporary pastime for him, until someone better came along.

I brooded for the rest of the day. Seeking consolation from my co-workers, all I got was ridicule. "A man buys a three hundred thousand dollar luxury condo for the two of you to live in and you're pissed at him," Darla said. "You're nuts!"

When I got off work, I ran to Dani knowing she would see my side.

"Doesn't that seem odd to you, I mean buying something so important without telling me?"

"Yes it seems odd, because he took you with him to look at the house before he rented it. Why didn't he do the same with the condo?"

"See, that's exactly what I thought."

"I think I'd be upset too."

"Well, I'm more than upset. I've decided not to move into the condo. I think it's what he wants anyway."

"So you're breaking up with him?"

"No! We can still see each other; we just won't be living together anymore."

"So you're going to tell him you don't want to live with him anymore, but you still want to date him?"

"Yeah, what's wrong with that?"

"It's taking a step back in your relationship. I don't think he'll understand."

"If he doesn't I guess we'll break up. Either way, I'm not living in that condo!"

Colin moved into the new condo, and I rented a small

apartment. We continued to see each other, but not much. The logical side of me knew we were over then, that I had turned into another one of Colin's charity causes, but I held on. What we had together was going to end—of that I was certain. The only mystery remaining was when and how.

It was Sunday night and I was expecting Colin to pick me up at seven to go out for dinner. He was a punctual man. If he told me he was going to pick me up at seven, he showed up within five minutes before or after, so when seven-thirty rolled around and he still wasn't there, I knew something was wrong.

I tried his cell, his pager, and home phone, but there was no answer. Hours passed, with me calling him every few minutes. I was beginning to get worried. *Has he been in an accident?* I drove to the condo, but he wasn't home. I knew there was an explanation; maybe an emergency at the hospital. Tomorrow I would find out. I fell asleep on the sofa.

The next morning I had to go in to work. As soon as I got there, I phoned Colin's office. The receptionist said he was with a patient but, would call me back later. In about an hour, I was paged to the phone. It was him.

"Hello, Tuesday," he said, in a dismal tone.

"Are you okay? What happened to you last night?"

His silence over the phone was telling. "Tuesday, I've done something awful," he said in a feeble voice. "I have betrayed your trust."

Even when Colin screwed up he had a way of making it sound high-class. I knew our relationship was dying. But another woman? I never saw her coming.

"Were you with her last night?"

"Will you ever forgive me?"

"Forgive you? You didn't belch, Colin, you cheated!"

"It was a lousy thing to do, letting you wait for me. I should have told you."

"How long has it been going on?"

"Last night was the first time, I swear."

"You expect me to believe that?"

"No. I don't expect you to believe anything I say."

"Who is she?"

"She's a nurse."

"Well that's classic."

"Listen, sweetheart, I don't want to talk about this anymore on the phone. I'll come by your place tonight."

"How do I know you're not going to stand me up again?"

"I'll be there this time."

Aunt Macy had an annoying way of pointing out the positive in the worst of situations. After Grandma Storm's funeral, in the stillness of our living room, surrounded by tuna casseroles, trays of rubbery celery, and sliced cheese with curled edges, Aunt Macy scanned the roomful of sullen-faced loved-ones and said, "We can all take solace in knowing Mother is no longer suffering." When I finally escaped Mama's twisted cruelty, Aunt Macy picked me up from the bus station, and on the drive to her house, she consoled me by saying, "Well at least you got out."

Maybe she was on to something. When I was a kid and Mama was forcing my head under bathwater, pushing and pushing, until I thought I was going to die, suddenly, I had a burst of strength and was able to fight her off, despite her almost 100 pound weight advantage. I could have easily drowned that day, and she may have even gotten away with killing me, by saying it was an accident. But in Aunt Macy's way of thinking, I *didn't* drown. I *survived*.

Years later, Mama installed a chain lock with a buzzer on the outside of my bedroom door. Driven by hunger, by some miracle, using a wire clothes hanger and blindly probing through a three inch opening from inside my room, I released the chain without setting off the buzzer. Most people would have seen being locked in a room, hungry with nothing but a bare bed and a bucket to pee in, as the armpit of bad luck. But not Aunt Macy. If she'd been there she would have said, "You're lucky you had that wire hanger."

As I sat in my apartment waiting for Colin to arrive, I wondered what Aunt Macy would do in my situation. *How would she deal with Colin's cheating ass?* He had been unfaithful, plain and simple, and our relationship was over. Losing Colin was a great loss. He had treated me better than any man I'd ever known, including my father. Especially my father. But hey, on the bright side, I'd lived in a sprawling home on a golf course, vacationed in

Hawaii, acquired a computer, a set of luggage, and some pretty swanky jewelry. *So things aren't so bad; right?*

Colin came by my apartment like he said he would, on time, like the old Colin. We talked in circles until the early hours of morning, resolving nothing. There was nothing to resolve. We were over. When he left that night, I knew I'd never see him again.

A few days later, I got an email from him: *I'm not prepared to break it off with you,* he wrote. He wasn't happy with his new relationship, or else he wouldn't have been contacting me. I'd given him an easy out, and he'd chosen not to take it. *Maybe there's a chance for us to be together again,* I thought.

We began emailing each other several times a day. He couldn't let go and neither could I. The emails led to visits. The visits let to sex. The sex led to confusion. This went on for weeks. Then I found out he was still seeing the nurse. Apparently he wasn't "prepared to break it off" with her either.

I'd had enough of being trailed along, so I decided to take action. Crazy action, but still it was action. I made copies of the steamy email correspondence between Colin and me, looked up the address of the nurse he was seeing in the phone book, and mailed them to her. *That ought to do it,* I thought. Without a doubt, I knew, after he'd found out I'd exposed him to the other women, he would despise me, and in a fit of rage, stomp the last breath out of our sick relationship.

Never in a million years would I have guessed he would call and thank me for helping him to break away from the nurse, and then ask me out to dinner. That's when I figured out why the thought of losing him upset me so much, why I couldn't let go. It was the coward in him I was most attracted to, his fear of confrontation. I'd dated other men similar to my daddy, but Colin *was* Daddy.

We drug our break-up out until both of us started seeing someone else. He found and married the love of his life, while I charged head on into one of the biggest mistakes of mine.

STORMY SKIES FOR TUESDAY

NOT LONG ENOUGH after my breakup with Colin, I started seeing Jerry, a pleasant-looking, respectable man eleven years my senior. He was a dentist and he lived in a condo in a golfing community. Playing armchair psychologist, I asked myself, *Is it a coincidence I'm dating another doctor who lives in a golfing community, or did I seek Jerry out in attempt to fix the mistakes I'd made with Colin?*

After dating only a few months, Jerry and I began planning our wedding in the Bahamas. Common sense told me we were moving too fast, and that I shouldn't get married so soon after breaking up with Colin. But I couldn't come up with a good enough reason *not* to marry Jerry. He was such a nice man. A good man. I hadn't tried one of those yet. I'd been too busy dating my daddy. Besides, it was time for me to remarry. Middle age was sneaking up behind me. Never mind being in love; I'd resigned myself to believing deep fondness and respect was the closest I was going to get.

Jerry took care of all the expenses for the wedding in the Bahamas, and I paid for a reception we had at the country club upon our return. I wanted to do my part financially, to prove to Jerry what his friends were insinuating—that I'd married him for his money—wasn't true. After honeymooning in the Bahamas, I moved into Jerry's condo in a gated golfing community that had a breathtaking view of the seventeenth hole. Was this also a coincidence, or was moving backward on the golf course a sign I was also moving backward in my life?

My marriage to Jerry was shaky from jump. He had two Lhasa Apso dogs that hated me for invading their territory. I could tell because they kept peeing on my side of the bed, and chewing my shoes. Jerry thought the dogs were two furry angels, but I knew better, because when he wasn't around they showed their teeth and growled at me.

As soon as Jerry came home from work every day, he got on the treadmill, and then he played with his dogs, and if there was any time left, he spent it with me. When I complained that he wasn't paying me enough attention, he bought me jewelry, or sent me flowers to placate me. But our problems were not entirely his fault. I was every bit as much to blame, because I didn't care enough to make the effort to work things out between us.

To cope with Jerry's rejection, I started obsessively rearranging the furniture in our condo. Every day when he got home he griped because the sofa or the bed would be in a different place. I couldn't stop my marriage from spinning down the drain, but furniture I could control.

I started going out to dinner and drinks with friends and co-workers after work. Once, when I'd had a few too many glasses of wine, I decided to spend the night at a friend's house and drive home in the morning.

"Where were you last night?" Jerry asked the following afternoon when he got home from work.

"Why do you ask? You obviously don't care, because you didn't even call," I said. "Tell me, Jerry, how long were you home yesterday before you noticed I wasn't here?"

"You didn't call *me* either."

"But I didn't call you on purpose to see if you would worry about me."

"Oh, so you were playing a game."

"No… well, maybe. I know it was probably wrong, and if you cared anything at all about me, it may have even been cruel. But I proved my point. For all you knew, I could have been in a car wreck, or raped and murdered, lying dead on the side of the road somewhere!"

"Well that certainly would have made my life a lot easier."

Anger is a powerful emotion. It made me shove Chad out of the trailer in the snow face-first. It made him pull a rifle on me and his own daughter. Anger pushes people to do and say all kinds of things they don't mean. But in a marriage, no matter how mad you are, there are lines you don't cross, words you're not allowed to say. Among them: I don't love you anymore. I no longer find you attractive, and I wish you were dead.

"I cannot believe you just said you wished I were

dead. I've had some mean things said to me in my life-time, but that's one of the worst. I wouldn't say that to an enemy, let alone my spouse."

"I didn't say I wished you were dead!"

"You implied it! That's close enough for me!"

I expected Jerry to try to take back what he'd said when he realized how much it hurt me. A man who loved me would have. But then a man who loved me wouldn't have said something so vicious in the first place. Instead of taking it back he elaborated. "Well it's true if you think about it. My life *has* been more difficult since you came along."

In that instant, I knew Jerry was not he man with whom I would spend the rest of my life. What he'd said catapulted me back to my abusive childhood and sent Mama's words reverberating in my head: *I hate you! You ruin everything! I wish you'd never been born!*

Looking at him standing in the kitchen drinking some sort of protein shake, I realized how unattractive I now found him. He looked young for his age, but his face appeared plastic. I'd always suspected he'd had a face-lift. How could I have married someone so self-absorbed? I stared him square in the eyes and gritted my teeth. "You're going to be sorry you ever said that! I can't even stand to look at you anymore!" I screamed, as I stormed off.

That night I slept in the guest room. In the coming weeks, Jerry sent so many flower arrangements to me at work, the furniture store began to look like a funeral home. But there was no winning me back. Our marriage was over. I was leaving him, that I knew for sure, as surely I'd known I was going to one day leave Chad the second he threatened to shoot Molly and me. But this time it wouldn't take me ten years. There were no children involved and I made enough money to at least support myself.

Within a couple of weeks, I'd filed for a divorce from Jerry and made plans to move back in with Dani and Barry until I'd saved enough money to get an apartment. Hitting the dead end of another relationship, I swore I was done with men, and made a vow to never get married again.

EMERGENCE

September, 2001

O N A SUNDAY evening, after a long day of slow sales at the furniture store, I decided to join some of my co-workers for dinner at a sports bar and grill.

At the restaurant, I slipped off my heels under the table, and sipped on a glass of the house chardonnay. As I pondered the menu, I wondered if I would ever look at food like a normal person. If I would ever be able to open a can of beans without the cube of fatty pork floating at the top reminding me of the slabs of hog jowl Mama had forced me to eat as a child. Would I ever stop shuddering at the sight of cottage cheese, because of my memory of having to drink curdled milk? And even after so many years of knowing the privilege of a full belly, each time I sat down to eat, I still recalled the hungry days, days of eating anything I could lay my hands on. Days when I dug through the trash for a stale crust of bread peppered with cigarette ashes, and was delighted when—while on my knees cleaning the kitchen floor—I happened upon a soggy Cheerio that had spilled from one of my brothers' overflowing breakfast bowls.

I ordered the chicken quesadilla and a salad. As usual, I ate every bite. I couldn't walk away from a table and leave a morsel of food on my plate, and sometimes I had to fight the urge to clean the plates of the people around me.

As we were leaving the restaurant, Judy, one of my co-workers, spotted a former high school boyfriend and asked me if I would go over to his table with her so she could say hello. I agreed to, because Judy was a good lady, plus she'd given me a ride to the restaurant.

When Judy and I approached the table, a smile of recognition painted her classmate's face as he stood to embrace her. Judy turned to me. "Travis, this is my friend, Tuesday." Travis, in turn, introduced both Judy and me to his friend, whose name was Wally.

As soon as Travis said *Wally*, I almost giggled. I didn't know real people were named Wally. I thought it was a TV name reserved for actors playing the part of half-wit gas station attendants with grease-smudged faces and grimy fingernails. But this Wally was no grease monkey. He was tall, clean-cut and boyishly cute. He was wearing khaki shorts, a red polo, and the glow of a fresh sunburn on his cheeks, which he pointed out was from playing in a golf tournament earlier in the afternoon.

Judy and I stood awkwardly by their table for a few minutes, until Travis asked us to join them. While he and Judy reminisced about their high school days, I was left to make idle chat with Wally. No problem. I didn't have trouble carrying on a conversation with a stranger. It's what I did every day, and there was plenty to talk about in the wake of the terrorist bombing of the twin towers.

Wally's quick smile and thick southern accent put me at ease right off. If his attitude could have spoken it would have said, I don't care what people think of me. I am a nice, southern guy, therefore I will act like a nice, southern guy. This is who I am. It was refreshing after having been around fake salespeople all day.

As Wally told me he was from Georgia, and went on to explain how he ended up in Indiana, I thought, *if I was looking to date someone, I might be interested in this guy.* But I wasn't looking. After a long string of flops, I was over trying to have a relationship.

Wally ordered a beer for himself and a glass of wine for me. In the next three hours we spent together, we played shuffleboard and he let me win. We had another drink. He took one of my hands in his and said it was the prettiest he'd ever seen. I blushed. Time sped by. Around midnight, he excused himself, saying he had to be at work early. We said our goodbyes and he left the restaurant. *What a nice guy,* I thought, as he walked away.

Less than five minutes later, I sensed someone standing behind me and glanced back over my shoulder. It was Wally. "Well hello, again," I said. "Forget something?"

He stood there grinning. "Something told me to come back in," he said.

Any other guy, to spare his male ego, might have made up an excuse for coming back, told me he'd left his keys, or forgot to leave a tip. But Wally didn't need to make an excuse; his grin said it all. We both knew the *something* that made him come back into the restaurant was me.

After about thirty more minutes of conversation, he got up and said goodbye again. "I *have* to go home this time."

"Oh, I understand. I've got to work in the morning too." I said. "We'll be leaving soon, if I can drag Judy away from Travis."

I walked with Wally to the door and watched him get into his car. Before I'd even made it back to our table, he appeared beside me again. We both laughed.

"I have a daughter. She's seven," he blurted the minute we sat down at the table.

"Well I have a daughter *and* a son," I blurted right back. "Nineteen and fifteen."

"You don't look old enough to have teenagers."

"I started young."

We talked only a few more minutes, long enough to exchange phone numbers and email addresses. I walked with him out to his car. When we got there, right before he got in, he leaned over and kissed me softly. It had all the excitement of a first kiss, and yet felt familiar, as if we had kissed before. This time he really left, and I went back into the restaurant and pulled Judy away from her classmate so we could go home.

The next day, I hoped Wally would call. I hoped he wouldn't call. I was not looking for another rebound relationship, or any relationship for that matter, but I couldn't seem to get him off my mind.

He didn't call. He was at work so he emailed instead: *Can we meet for a drink later and maybe play a game or two of pool?*

I gave his invitation some thought. *What would be the harm of playing pool?* "One date—and that's it," I told myself, as I typed the email confirming the time we were to meet.

But as these things go, one date became two, and two dates turned into cozy dinners at his apartment. *I'm only dating him,* I reassured myself. *It's not like I'm going to marry the guy.* Still, I was relieved to find out he was not a doctor, or dentist, or in any way connected to the medical field. He was an accountant. An accountant with a grease monkey's name.

Soon Wally and I were together almost every night of the week. His weekends were reserved for his daughter, Sydney, and that was okay with me because it left me free to see Molly and Daryl. After we'd been dating for about a month, he decided he wanted me to meet Sydney, and invited me to go to the movie theater with them. I asked Daryl to join us, but according to him, going to the movies with his mom was no longer a cool thing to do.

Sydney was a tiny blond angel, with the same open, take-me-or-leave-me personality as her dad, minus the southern accent. I found this out on our third trip to the ladies room after she'd drunk a giant soft drink. She looked up at me with bodacious hazel eyes and said, matter of factly, "Sorry, I have to *go* so much; I'm a pee-er.

You'll just have to deal with it." From that moment on I was putty in her hands.

Sometime during my search for an apartment, I thought maybe I should buy a house instead of continuing to throw my money away on rent. This was part of the sensible accountant way of thinking I'd picked up from being around Wally. Under his guidance, I went to the bank and got pre-approved for a loan up to $110,000, but to keep my budget comfortable, he suggested I look at houses in the price range of $100,000 or less.

When I started house hunting my spirit got dampened right away. The houses in my price range were older places with sloping roofs in iffy neighborhoods. Inside they were even worse—fruit patterned wallpaper, avocado green appliances and uneven floors. When I'd almost given up on having a place of my own, Wally suggested I ask my realtor to show me condos. He thought I would be more likely to find something in my price range. At that point, I liked him so much if he had told me I should live in a cardboard box, I would have considered it.

It didn't take me long to find a condo in a great part of town, $13,000 under my budget limit. The place was small, but had tons of charm with its corner fireplace and vaulted ceiling. There were two bedrooms and a loft that could be used as a bedroom for when the kids came, although Daryl was the only one who needed one because Molly was now going to college and had moved into an apartment with a friend.

Wally and I were on our first camping trip together, roughing it with a tent, a couple of sleeping bags and some bratwurst. We were sitting by the fire toasting marshmallows for s'mores. Wally had chocolate in the corners of his mouth, and a flickering flame mirrored in his eyes. Suddenly the time seemed right to tell him about my childhood, but I wasn't sure how to bring the subject up. Child abuse is not something easily slipped into casual conversation.

"Did I tell you I was planning on writing a book someday?" I asked.

"Oh yeah? That's cool. What about?"

"It's going to be based on a true story about my child-hood. You see, I was abused by my mother."

His eyes grew large. "Wow." he said, gently. "I'm so sorry that happened to you."

"She did some crazy things to me. And here's the strange part: I was the only kid of five she treated that way."

"Why?"

"That's the million dollar question. I wanted to believe it was because of a brain injury, but later found out that wasn't the case at all."

"But she *has* to be mentally ill."

"Or narcissistic and just plain mean."

"Either way, it sounds like a story that needs to be told.

Good for you for writing a book." He pulled me in close to him. "Do you want to talk about what happened?"

"No, not tonight. I only wanted you to know."

Not long after I closed on the condo, Wally and I met for a late dinner after I got off work.

"I bought a bottle of wine to celebrate you buying your first home," he said after we'd finished eating.

"That's so sweet!"

"I'll bring it over."

"Tonight?"

"Yeah, I'll follow you to your condo."

Follow me? Bad idea. I still hadn't gotten used to driving to the condo, and I lost my way almost every time. But I hadn't told Wally about my problem yet.

"You know what, we're having a big sale at the store tomorrow, and I really should get to bed early."

"It's only eight o'clock. I won't stay long. You'll be in bed by ten."

"Okay. I guess I'll see you there then," I said. Then we parted ways to go to our cars.

As I got behind the wheel, my heart pounded and I could feel my dinner inching up my throat. I was so shook up I wasn't even sure which way to pull out of the parking lot. I wanted to go left, but I had my doubts. I decided to use Dani's mother's trick and go the opposite of what I thought. I turned right. In the rearview mirror, I saw Wally pull out behind me.

I saw a stoplight ahead. *I think I turn right—no left—at*

the light. I got in the left lane and hit my blinker. Wally did the same. Halfway down the road, I realized I was going the wrong way, so I turned left on the first side street with the intention of circling back around to the light. Once I was on the side street, I turned left again onto a another side street, still on a mission to find my way back to the light where I'd made my first wrong turn. In the rearview, I saw Wally flashing his bright lights. *Oh, crap!* I pulled over.

He got out of his car and walked toward me, a frown on his face. "Where the hell are you going?"

"To the condo."

"Well it must be a way I've never been before, because your condo is on the east side of town and you're going west."

I hated when people talked direction to me. He may as well been speaking a foreign language. "I am?"

"First you turn the wrong way at the light, and then you start going down all kinds of strange side roads. Hey, if you're trying to lose me just say so and I'll be on my way."

"I'm *not* trying to lose you, Wally!" I pleaded. "I got lost!"

"You expect me to believe you got lost going somewhere you go every day? Bullshit! I don't need this! I'm going home!" He got in his car and drove off.

Watching him disappear in the night, I started crying. *Way to go, Tuesday. You and your messed up head just ruined another relationship.*

When I left home and moved in with Aunt Macy, the time that immediately followed was difficult and confusing. Imagine you've been in a bad car wreck, one that would have killed most people, but you somehow manage to come out of it with no serious injuries other than some deep cuts across your face. You're well aware of your injuries, but you don't concern yourself with them right away, because you're too grateful to be alive. After the doctor stitches you up and gives you some medication, you go home and continue your life, unaware of the true extent of the damage that has been done to you. And then the day arrives when the bandages come off, and you look in the mirror and realize your face is covered with jagged scars—scars you're going to have to contend with for the rest of your life. After I left home, for a short period of time, I was so grateful to be free of Mama's cruelty—grateful to be alive—I thought maybe I'd come through it all okay. But that was before I saw the scars.

Around this time was when I began documenting the trauma of my early childhood as it came back to me in nightmares and sudden flashes. After I'd written down each gruesome flashback, I folded the paper, put it in my box of memories, and then stored the box under my bed. This ritual seemed to help me cope, and once I'd symbolically put a memory away, it seldom revisited me. As an adult, every now and then, I took out the pictures and looked at them, but never went back to read the memories I'd written. Now after years of Dani's gentle nudging, and with the help of the these fragments of my secret past, I was ready to began "the book."

At first I wrote with ferocity and determination, but after only a few months, I hit a wall. Before I could continue, I needed to somehow impart meaning and purpose to what had happened to me as a child, to, in my mind, make my story something more than a pointless reflection of human suffering. Pointless, because the most important question had not yet been answered: Why did my mother single me out from all her other children to abuse? Deep down, because I didn't know the answer, I still thought it was somehow my fault, and I harbored a sense of self-badness and shame. I knew unless I found the answer I could never finish the book.

My story was like an injured animal, and the place where I stopped writing dangled like its broken leg. It languished in my laptop for several months as an unfinished Word document before I decided to turn to research. I spent hours on the Internet combing through countless newspaper articles about abused children, in search of one similar to mine. After weeks of research, I ran across a story about a four year old girl who had been brutally beaten to death by her mother. Reading on, I found out that in the years before her death, the little girl had been severely mistreated over an extended period of time, whereas her five brothers were never harmed. In the article, she was referred to as a "scapegoat child," a term sometimes used by social workers.

Now, I had something to work with. I typed, *scapegoat child* in the search engine of my computer and came upon more stories of children who were the only ones in their families singled out for maltreatment. I learned the scapegoat child phenomenon is well-documented among child welfare experts, and surprisingly common, but like with all cases of child abuse, we don't hear much about it until the death of one of the children makes the papers. These findings convinced me I had been a scapegoat child, but still, my question had not been answered. Why did my mother choose *me* as her scapegoat and not one of my brothers?

I learned through further research that the family scapegoat is usually the most sensitive and most vulnerable of all the children, and often the one who reminds the abusive parent of something within herself she cannot accept. I, being a girl, was more sensitive and vulnerable than my male siblings, and also the one who reminded my mother of her other female child who had died. Mama most likely blamed herself for allowing Audrey to catch the polio virus, but the burden of that blame was too much for her to bear alone.

I was a scapegoat child, born of my mother's need to blame something outside herself for all the awful things that had happened to her, chosen to take on her guilt, shame, and feelings of inadequacy. This was my answer, my truth—or as close as I was ever going to get. I returned to my writing with insight and purpose.

BURYING THE ANGER

December, 2012

A MAN WAS DEFINITELY in the house. Lying in bed, still fuzzy with sleep, I could smell the soapy steam from his shower, hear the tap of his razor on the side of the sink. The smells and sounds of a man getting ready for the day reminded me of Daddy, and the mornings of my childhood spent waiting for him to come to my bed and give me a good morning kiss. Seeing him was what I lived for then. But one day he stopped coming. One day they all stopped coming.

Love, although elusive in my life, had always been a source of fascination to me. Because of my children, Aunt Macy, and Dani, I had loved absolutely, and experienced the soul-deep satisfaction of having my love returned. But I had never been *in love,* and I was bewildered by this powerful, mysterious state of the heart that makes people abandon their pride and surrender to someone without a second thought. Over the years, I'd often asked Dani,

"How do you know when you're really in love?" Her answer was always the same. "If you have to ask then you haven't been there yet."

The man who was now in my bathroom had solved the mystery. In the days after we met, I discovered when you're in love, like Dani had said, there is no doubt, no wondering *Is this it?* You know the instant of surrender. For me, that instant was the night we met when he came back into the restaurant the second time. The way he acted on an impulse, with confidence—seizing the opportunity without worrying what anyone thought—spoke to my heart. Eleven years earlier, I swore I'd never get married again. Now I lay in bed waiting for my husband's good morning kiss.

It took some serious talking to make Wally understand my problem with direction, and to convince him I wasn't trying to lose him the night he was following me to the condo. But eventually he came around. Sometimes I couldn't believe he was *still* around. In the beginning, my inability to trust and fear of rejection had tried to chase him away. Had he not been so patient, so consistent, so persevering, and had he not believed in us as a couple, I might have unconsciously destroyed our relationship as I'd done with others before. Of everything I had to conquer, as part of my healing, learning to trust was by far the most difficult. He was the first man who ever made me secure enough to give up my heart.

A breath of a kiss brushed across the side of my neck. "Good morning, beautiful." Wally and I had been together since the first night we met, and every day I woke up to the quiet confidence that he would always be there to give me a good morning kiss. "You should start getting ready," he said. "We'll need to be on the road soon."

There was an odd sense of calmness about me as I dressed for the funeral. Through the years I'd often speculated how I would react to the news of Mama's death. *How much relief am I allowed to feel? How much grief is expected?* Mama was dead. The source of my fear was dead. Did that mean my fear itself was now dead? The creator of my anger was about to be buried. But would the lingering remnants of that anger be buried too?

At the showing, Mama's casket remained closed, because she'd been dead in her home for a while before anyone found her and her body had begun to decay. On a table beside her casket, in an oval Victorian frame, was a photograph of her as a young woman. It was the way she looked the first time she told me she hated me, as she struck me with the wire end of a fly swatter. I had since forgotten the sting of the wire, but the words would be with me forever.

Staring at her photograph, I wondered if near the end she'd had a moment of regret. Thinking of her alone, kneeling in a dark corner begging for the chance to go back, reach back, take back the horrible things she had done made me bury my face in my hands and cry. *If you were faced with such a moment, Mama, my heart aches for you. If you weren't my heart aches for you.*

313

Wally put his arm around me to show his support, as I turned to address the family members now approaching me. My siblings and I engaged in an obligatory stiff hug, and then went our separate ways. I wondered, as I looked at their children, how my brothers would explain the new aunt that had suddenly appeared. Molly and Daryl didn't come to the funeral; they had never known Mama as a grandmother, but I'd heard my brothers' children had a relationship with her.

Now that my book was published revealing the secrets of Mama's past, what would my brothers tell their children when they are old enough to read it and ask questions? To try to spare them this dilemma, I took Dani's advice and changed all the names in the book, but people have a way of finding things out. If they do, there are only two possible answers. Either Mama Rose was a deeply troubled, mentally ill woman, or their aunt Tuesday is evil for writing such awful lies about their grandmother. Which would they choose?

Mama was dead. While she lived there lived hope—a glimmer of chance—we would somehow find a way to put our hideous past behind us and reconcile. Now my dream of hearing her call me Tuesday again would not be realized, and she was never going to explain why she mistreated me. She had left no answers behind. From relatives who had gone through her personal belongings, I'd learned she'd left no journal or un-mailed letters. There was nowhere left to turn but to the enigma that remained: my mother was disturbed in a way that neither I, nor anyone else, could explain, and for reasons I would never fully understand, she stopped loving me, if she ever did. But this I could finally accept, because now I knew what love felt like.

There's truth to what they say—that in death all is forgiven. When I was a child, I believed Daddy when he promised to rescue me from my daily abuse and when he didn't, in many ways, his was the greater betrayal. Not until after his death was I able to forgive him and let go of my resentment. Now Mama was gone, and the time had come to rid myself of the remaining shards of anger still jutting from my heart. At her funeral, realizing death truly is the ultimate closure, I forgave her too. Forgave her for robbing me of my childhood, for the years of torment, and for dismissing what she'd done without accountability, which turned out to be the most damaging blow of all. I forgave my mother even though she had never asked for my forgiveness, or admitted she'd done anything for which to be forgiven. I forgave her for myself.

EPILOGUE

I T'S MY OPINION that no one comes away from severe childhood trauma unscathed. Every child we allow to be abused today has the potential to grow into a defective adult. Yesterday's victims, at their worst, are convicts, drug addicts, or abusive parents. At best, they appear normal to the outside world, living anonymously among us as our neighbors, friends, and co-workers, while silently struggling with the damage in their own private ways.

Some of the scars from my childhood trauma remain with me today. My ability to trust has been fractured, because I know, first hand, evil can exist even behind seemingly kind faces. I still have bouts with depression and a tendency toward reclusiveness. The phobias and fears that plagued my young adulthood continue to linger below the surface of my conscious mind. I'm still afraid of driving, especially on an interstate or in a big city, and I still get lost regularly. I can't submerge my head in water, and when I feel my life slipping from my control, I do something I can control—I rearrange furniture.

But the most devastating damage of all, is that I've missed out on the joy of family. I grew up without a mother or a father, and the isolation from my siblings during our childhood has carried over into our adult lives. I see one of my brothers and his wife and kids once a year. I have no contact with any other family members. Still, my life is filled with love and support. I have the family I created, my friends and in-laws, and they all mean the world to me.

After failing to get back in touch with Aunt Macy, I later found out she had passed away. Of all the mistakes I had to resolve during that arduous time of my life, not contacting her proved to be the most excruciating of all. But as Aunt Macy herself—forever the optimist— would have pointed out, I have learned many life lessons from my experiences. One of the most valuable is this: Children—and perhaps the elderly—are the only true victims of abuse. As adults, we are only victims when we allow ourselves to be. The instant we make the decision to strike back, we become warriors. When the fight is over, we will have either won or lost, but one thing is for sure, we will not have been victims.

ABOUT THE AUTHOR

LEIGH BYRNE IS an American author who lives in southern Indiana. *Call Me Cockroach* is her second book. Her first book, *Call Me Tuesday,* was published in 2012, and is available through Amazon. To find out more about Leigh, visit her blog: http://callme2sday.blogspot.com/